One Size
Does Not
Fit All

One Size Does Not Fit All

Diversity in the Classroom

RANDY HOWE, EDITOR

KAPLAN)

PUBLISHING

New York

© 2010 Randy Howe

Published by Kaplan Publishing, a division of Kaplan, Inc.
1 Liberty Plaza, 24th Floor
New York, NY 10006

Printed in the United States of America

10 9 8 7 6 5 4 3 2 1

Library of Congress Cataloging-in-Publication Data has been applied for.

ISBN-13: 978-1-60714-115-0

Kaplan Publishing books are available at special quantity discounts to use for sales promotions, employee premiums, or educational purposes. For more information or to purchase books, please call the Simon & Schuster special sales department at 866-506-1949.

Dedication

For my godsons, Sean and John. May their teachers be as dedicated, thoughtful, and empathetic as those that took the time to contribute to this book.

CONTENTS

INTRODUCTION:
THE LESSON'S OBJECTIVE

WHEN GIVEN A class roster, the teacher sees a list of names. Each name represents a child, a mind and a heart yet to be discovered; an amalgam of background, experiences, and learning style. The class roster is a starting place, but soon thereafter the teacher meets each student, and somewhere between receiving the roster and that moment of greeting, he or she will want to prepare for any special needs those students might have. As the year progresses, the teacher will certainly learn more about each child's strengths and weaknesses, and this will factor into the myriad decisions that must be made on a daily basis. There are so many details to keep track of, so many choices to make, but this is the life of the professional educator. I know that I have learned to proceed with care, to try to remove myself from the equation and put the student first, because to fail to do so is to rob a child of the respect that he or she deserves. The bottom line is, no one has to face up to the issues of diversity more than teachers.

In the past, the United States has been less of a melting pot and more of a salad bowl as people of varying backgrounds coexisted but didn't necessarily intermingle. Take a walk down any school hallway today and you will begin to wonder if the melting pot analogy isn't making a comeback. Step inside any classroom and you will see that it most certainly is. Not only are different kinds of kids hanging out together, but they are learning together. This is especially good news for someone like me, who teaches special education and lives by the creed of "the least restrictive environment." By this, I mean the idea that special needs students should be placed in classes in which they are able to receive as much individualized instruction as possible while still learning alongside their peers. Done properly, inclusion is a wonderful opportunity for all.

One Size Does Not Fit All goes beyond discussions of least restrictive environment and race, however. Just as special education has moved out of the basement to claim its rightful place among all the other classes, students with alternative lifestyles are feeling a greater level of comfort and support as they come out of the closet. Two stories, written by Jeff Ballam and Damian Bariexca, deal with issues of personal identity with respect to sexual orientation and gender. This topic was worthy of a cover story, in the September 2009 *New York Times Magazine* and is certainly worthy of a place in this book. Guiding a group of students through a school year is rarely a smooth experience, but these two stories offer more optimism than the reader might have predicted.

Autism has also come to the forefront of educational discussions over the past decade, and in "The Memorable

One," Stephanie Bell writes about her kindergarten class and, in particular, a Japanese-American student named Takehiro. To read about their field trip and the way this child broke the rules to make contact with an intriguing art exhibit is to experience the feelings of consternation and joy that make those most challenging of students so unforgettable.

On that note, there are plenty of stories about behavioral issues in *One Size*. Good choices, bad choices, the success of each teacher's day hinges on the behavior of the students, and as we all know, just one or two kids can ruin a lesson. Shawna Messina's "The Bodyguard" is a good example of how one child can help raise up a class while another, improperly placed and undersupported, can threaten to tear it all down. Cathryn Soenksen warns us about making assumptions when she recalls her year with Miguel in "First Row, Second Seat Back." There is also "Pockets Full of Poker Chips," in which Randy Howe realizes he must expand his capacity for empathy in the face of student conflict. Dr. Kathy Briccetti writes about a similar effort at conflict management, but from the perspective of a school psychologist, in "The Power of One." The detailing of what it takes to improve student behavior continues with Erica C. Aguirre and her student Joey in "Unconditional Dedication"; with Dr. Rebecca Branstetter and Darren in "The Invisible Knapsack"; with Anne Dandridge Conrad and a little girl named Becky in "Something's Gotta Give"; and with Megan Highfill and Jasmine, whose behavior is challenging but in a whole different way, in

"Anthem." Important life lessons are learned every day in schools, Ms. Highfill teaches us, even in music class.

The students in this book come from diverse backgrounds, and so do the contributors. Dr. Susan DeMersseman, Anne Dandridge Conrad, and Dr. Rebecca Branstetter are all school psychologists, and sometimes their goal is to evaluate a student's strengths and weaknesses, while other times it is to counsel them on matters that are literally of life and death. On the theme of diverse educators, there is even a contribution from a basketball coach. Amy Cummings-Barnabi confides, in "Color Outside the Lines," that sometimes you have to push aside all the advice and research and just go with your gut instinct. It is a lesson that definitely has classroom implications. Several stories take us abroad, as Susan Laughlin contrasts American and Japanese cultures in her story, "The Nail That Sticks Up Gets Hammered Down," while Lisa Santilly writes about working with deaf and hard of hearing students in Toronto in "When Dogs Can Talk." Amy Beth Blumstein's "The Power of Words" is an amazing story of teacher perseverance in the face of parental pressure set in post-9/11 London. All three stories touch on the theme of breaking down old walls with new ideas, as does Madeline Sanchez's "*La Oportunidad.*" Ms. Sanchez's story, along with Erica C. Aguirre's "Unconditional Dedication," details the daily efforts made by teachers to undo the "separate but equal" mistakes of a salad-bowl society. In both cases, the accountability begins, surprisingly enough, not with some outside agitator, but with the students themselves.

Cultural diversity seems, at first glance, to be central to Allison Anderson's "What My Students Taught Me" and Kerstin Rowe's "Beyond Boxes: How Today's Students Disable Labels." In the end, though, each story states the case for having faith in kids and their ability to talk their way, and even joke their way, through prejudice and the ill-conceived efforts of adults to address issues of diversity. In the process, the talking and the joking accomplish the mission in ways the teacher never could have predicted, let alone those in the ivory tower.

As a special education teacher, I was drawn to the stories told by regular education teachers working hard to address the needs of all their students. Much like Ms. Rowe in "Beyond Boxes," Patricia M. Castellone does her best to respond professionally and enthusiastically when handed a district initiative to increase diversity awareness in her students. In "The Star, A Heart Within," she writes about a little boy who ends up giving her lesson the kind of closure every teacher hopes for. Similarly, another little boy helps Johanna Chesser to see the benefits of welcoming a needy student into the classroom, even if he comes along with support staff. Her special education co-teacher is just one of the many heroes to appear in this collection, and the title of Ms. Chesser's tale, "Oh Yes, He Can!" just as easily could have been "Oh Yes, She Did!"

In "What My Students Taught Me," Ms. Anderson writes, "I am a lifelong learner. That's why I teach." This notion is central to many of the stories, but none more so than Megan J. Koonze's "Teens on the High Seas." From Ms. Koonze, teachers receive all the inspiration they will ever need to chaperone overnight field trips! Read and learn how a couple of days of working on a one-hundred-foot schooner helped a freshman girl with ADHD blossom. In "Steven and Me," Dr. Samuel R. Bennett also shows how the efforts we make outside of the regular school day can often be precisely what the child needs. A student becomes more like a family member, and in the end everyone benefits.

Although this book consists of twenty-three inspiring, thought-provoking stories, it was never intended to be merely anecdotal. There are practical lessons here as well—lessons that will hopefully have great influence on every reader's classroom. Dr. Mona Briggs's "Five Steps to Differentiation" is the pinnacle of practicality, with its best-practice suggestions, and that is why it is the final chapter. If *One Size* is like a lesson plan, "Five Steps" is its closure. There is also homework for the willing reader, as the book concludes with a list of reading questions. It is my hope that *One Size Does Not Fit All* will be used by educational leaders as part of their professional development sessions and by education professors as they prepare future teachers for life in the classroom. In thinking about these questions, the reader will bring his or her own meaning to each story. And through a discussion of this meaning with others, individual experience can become collective experience, and students will surely reap the rewards. That is the hope that drives *One Size*. It is the same hope that propelled the contributors to spend hours writing about their students and their craft.

In some ways we are all the same, and in some ways we are not. That is just fine as long as we never stop learning from, and about, one another. I have come to understand that this kind of work is sometimes difficult, but always worth the effort. To celebrate difference is nice, but to accommodate it is education as it was meant to be. It is to see teachers at their best. Our kids deserve nothing less.

— *Randy Howe*
Madison, Connecticut

■

SECTION ONE

THE LESSON

The Memorable One

Stephanie Bell

W HAT MAKES A child memorable? Is it his sweet smile? His intelligence and charm? His sense of humor? His courage to overcome obstacles? In this case, it is all of these things.

I remember meeting Takehiro. His brother, Ichiro, was in my kindergarten class. At dismissal, his mother stood outside the door, waiting with all the other mothers. I spied Mrs. Nakamura in the back, her tiny frame hidden by most of the other parents. From the doors, I heard the wailing before I saw it. As the other parents began to clear away, I became acutely aware that the screams were coming from the two-year-old twins Mrs. Nakamura desperately held, one on each hip. As they wiggled and howled, I wondered how she did it. Twins, both autistic. One of those little boys was Takehiro.

Three years later, Takehiro entered kindergarten. My class had always been an inclusion class, and I loved it that way. Teaching students with disabilities reminded me to celebrate the milestones, no matter how small they might be. Takehiro was different from my other students in two ways: He was autistic, and he came from a Japanese-speaking home. Takehiro had no spontaneous speech, a deep attachment to the color purple (a color reserved for royalty in Japan), and a strong will. Would Takehiro ever speak? Would he relate to the other children? Would they include him? I questioned how Takehiro could learn in English, when he heard only Japanese at home.

Initially, Takehiro struggled to have his way. When it was time to sit, he would squirm away and make vocalizations of distress. When it was time to write, he would run around the classroom. My goal was to give Takehiro a voice. Since it was unlikely that he would speak, I decided to teach him to write.

As a beginning teacher, I was offered my first assignment at an applied behavior analysis (ABA) preschool. This experience was priceless, as it gave me a whole repertoire of tools for my teaching toolbox. Being well trained in the ABA method of behavior modification, I utilized this strategy to shape Takehiro's behaviors. Using his beloved purple grapes as a reinforcer, I was able to teach Takehiro to sit down at the table during writing time. This sounds simple, but it was a long, uphill battle for this willful child. It took many months of successive approximations for Takehiro to be able to sit at the table appropriately. I began by task-analyzing what he would need to be successful at sitting down during writing time. First, he would need to be near the table. Each time he got closer, I reinforced him with bountiful praise and five seconds of play with his purple grapes. I also praised him for coming quietly to the table with a hair tousle and an exuberant, "Good boy, Takehiro!" Eventually, he was required to sit in the chair. When he did this without hurling himself off of it or vocalizing, he was praised and given the grapes. He learned to sit for short periods of time, and I would reward him with a walk around the classroom, since he craved movement. When this first goal was achieved, I put writing paper in front of him with a box of crayons. Since he had no spontaneous speech and little command of English, he often just wrote his name and scribbled in purple crayon. I praised him lavishly for each small achievement and celebrated his progress.

Although he was nonverbal, Takehiro demonstrated that he was smart in many different ways. He was able to point to letters when prompted, found pictures that began with presented sounds, played sound/symbol games, and even showed that he recognized certain words by matching words and pictures. This was my cue to push him further.

By midyear, in an effort to teach Takehiro more English words and to get him to attempt to write, I started giving him writing papers with pictures of objects and one blank line on the page. Takehiro's job was to write the name of the object on the line. Takehiro was echolalic, so he would repeat the name of the object, then write it.

After he mastered that, I started putting two lines for him below the picture. Takehiro had to write a descriptor and the name of the object—for example, "purple grapes" or "tall tree." I would provide a choice of descriptors, and he would select one. Most of the time he chose one of mine, but sporadically he would surprise me and write his own descriptor. Sometimes Takehiro would show me his playful side and write something funny, like "purple tree," which was always accompanied by a wicked grin.

We soon moved on to action photos. Takehiro would get two lines to write a noun and a verb, such as "boy running" or "fish swimming." I would ask Takehiro what was happening in the picture, and after shaping the behavior, he got used to providing the two-word phrases. Takehiro soon graduated to simple sentences. I would prompt him by asking what was happening in the picture and he would say, "Dog jumping." I would respond with, "Yes, that's right. The dog is jumping. Say that: 'The dog is jumping.'" Takehiro would repeat the full sentence, and in response, I praised him. I would point to each line as I slowly repeated the sentence, demonstrating one-to-one correspondence. He would then write that sentence on the four lines provided.

I soon began encouraging Takehiro to draw some of his own pictures. Of course, the purple theme ran deep. It was often the only color he would use. He began his drawings very simply. I would put three objects in front of him, and he would choose one to draw. His very first one was of his purple grapes (of course). The next one was of a strawberry. He would then tell me, with prompting, a simple sentence about the picture. I often repeated what he told me, adding the missing linking words to make it a complete sentence. I would write the appropriate number of lines, one for each word, then have Takehiro point to each space as he repeated the amended sentence. Next, he would write it. Within a short time, Takehiro's pictures were more elaborate, as well as from his mind rather than from a tangible object. One that stands out for me was the work he did following a field trip to the beach. He drew an intricate, colorful beach scene with all different types of shells (and the purple grapes). Below, he wrote, "We went to the beach. We saw pretty shells." Seeing this brought tears to my eyes. What a huge accomplishment for this little boy!

I invited Mrs. Nakamura to come and share Takehiro's wonderful progress. She broke down in sobs as she looked through the progression of writing samples. In her limited English, she thanked me with a quiet voice and a polite bow. Together, we celebrated Takehiro finding his voice.

While Takehiro made progress in the classroom academically, a little boy named Jake took him under his wing socially. Jake was one of the "cool kids." He was also a very compassionate and caring child. Jake was the youngest of five children and took pride in nurturing Takehiro and guiding him to do the right thing.

On the carpet, Jake sat next to Takehiro. He modeled the appropriate behaviors and gently told Takehiro,

"Takehiro, sit like this," or, "Takehiro, put your hands in your lap." Takehiro loved Jake right back, and they became inseparable.

Jake's acceptance of Takehiro was a model for the other children, and they quickly accepted him, too. The girls often fought over who got to hold Takehiro's hand when walking down the hall. Lunchtime was another opportunity for the class to assist Takehiro and help him be successful.

At recess, Jake would include Takehiro in the games. He would show him how to play and cheer him on in his attempts. The children would center games around Takehiro and his ability to play. They would adjust the rules for him so that he could be included. For example, kickball would include a gentle pitch and instructions to kick and run, with teammates and friends cheering him on and guiding him around the bases. Gleeful shouts would ring out across the playground: "Run to first! Now, go to second! Steal third! You're going all the way, Takehiro!" The ball was often held until Takehiro made it around, and high fives were delivered by all. On the occasion that he was tagged out, Takehiro continued to run anyway, with a huge grin and a victory dance at home plate.

Often, our morning meetings would center around messages of acceptance, empathy, and differences. Children at age five have a very keen moral compass. Our discussions were rich and full of ideas on how to embody these traits. My students were able to demonstrate these character traits through role-plays and then were reinforced when they used their knowledge in authentic situations. Takehiro was the beneficiary of much of their goodwill.

Takehiro also had a devilish side, which I found delightfully endearing. On a trip to an art museum, the children were reminded not to touch the exhibits. As we rounded a corner, there in the middle of the room was the most exciting exhibit in the museum. Takehiro couldn't take his eyes off it. It was a picnic table and bench that appeared to be covered in the most shiny, glossy, glittery, sparkly snow ever to be seen. It beckoned Takehiro to take a closer look. He wanted to touch it. He quickly glanced around to see if anyone was looking, then slowly stretched his arm out toward the glistening snow. The aide holding his other hand saw him and reminded him of the "no touching" rule. She started to guide Takehiro away from the exhibit, but with his eyes locked firmly on me and a smile planted on his face, he reached out to get a quick touch. But he was too late: He missed the exhibit. As he was led in the other direction, Takehiro put out a foot to try to make contact, until he was stretched out as long as he could extend. But still he could not reach. Finally, he broke away from the aide and gave a big, fat sweep across the bench of the picnic table. With a self-satisfied smile and a snicker, he went back to his aide. After witnessing the whole thing, I just had to turn away and laugh at his determination to touch that picnic table. This simple act gave me such joy because I felt as if I could see who Takehiro was inside. For a moment, it was as if the clouds lifted and his inner self came shining through. Gone was the disconnect that autistic children often display. He was related and typical. Those humorous times helped me see that Takehiro was special, and I knew he had touched my heart forever.

Over the course of the year, Takehiro grew both academically and socially. He was a vital part of our class and finished kindergarten with many friends. He was always asked to go on playdates, and children continued to vie for his attention. Academically, he made strides and overcame challenges that the special education team, his parents, and I thought were impossible. Overjoyed, we celebrated each triumph.

Although he accomplished more than we ever thought possible, Takehiro did not speak spontaneously that year. However, he did find his voice with his trusty purple crayon in one hand and grapes in the other. He wrote his stories and read them to us. He made friends and was accepted by his peers. His sense of humor brought delight to my classroom. I looked forward to seeing him daily, as every day with Takehiro was an adventure. I had never felt like a better teacher than when I taught Takehiro. I was lucky to have him in my class and honored to be his teacher.

It has been several years now since Takehiro left kindergarten. I have since started working in a new district. When Ichiro graduated from elementary school, I received an envelope thick with letters from Ichiro and Takehiro. I was thrilled to get the letters, especially Takehiro's. He wrote of his third-grade experience and how he missed me and had loved his kindergarten year. I found it amazing that he remembered me and his year in kindergarten. I know I will always remember Takehiro, his academic gains, and his charming smile. He was my first memorable student, and I will never forget him.

THE POWER OF WORDS

Amy Beth Blumstein

O N SEPTEMBER 11, 2001, the world changed forever. On September 12, 2001, *my* world as a teacher changed forever. Unlike most Americans, I was not living in the United States when the World Trade Center towers went down. Rather, I was teaching four- and five-year-old children in the inner city of London, England. My students were, for all intents and purposes, refugees from all around the world. Among the thirty-three students in my class, eight different languages were spoken, ranging from Bengali to tribal African languages to British English. As a Caucasian Jewish-American female, I too added to the diversity of the classroom. My students, although young, led difficult and challenging lives, and school had become a place of safety, security, and stability for all of them.

The afternoon of September 11 was winding down smoothly when two British mothers burst into my classroom. One went straight to me while the other helped my classroom aide with packing up the children. The one who addressed me could barely get her words out as she described the events that had occurred in New York City. I was dumbfounded and left dismissal in the hands of my aide and these parents while I went to my headmaster to get some more information. I also wanted to ask for permission to leave early to make sure my family was safe. My headmaster was curt in providing the news he had heard from the BBC. He told me to get in touch with my family in the United States on my own time and to be sure to return to work the following morning. Stunned by his abrupt response and already in shock by the news, I complied and left directly after dismissal, trying to get in touch with my family and friends in New York City.

Once I knew the details and that my family was safe, I broke down and mourned the loss of the day. But it was only for a few hours, for I was determined to return to school as per my headmaster's demands, without delay and with the utmost professionalism. Little did I know that the headmaster was the least of my worries.

As I opened the door to my classroom and started welcoming in the children for the day, I was greeted with supportive words of kindness from most of the parents. Having been at the school for a few years, I had become a part of the community, and it was refreshing to see that I had the support of these people. But as I greeted Ikram, a wonderful young Muslim boy whose family came from Bangladesh, he was unusually quiet. He scurried past me and joined his friends in the block corner, as he did every day.

When I said good morning to Inaam, Ikram's mother, who as usual was dressed in a burqa, she looked me in the eye and, using perfect British English, shouted, "You and your people got exactly what you deserved yesterday."

Certain I had not heard her correctly, I responded, "Pardon?"

"Yesterday," she continued. "The planes. I am behind those pilots and believe they did what was right. The Americans deserve to die." As her litany of reasons why she supported the actions of the previous day continued, she became more visibly angry with me. Inaam's words were severe and clear, and they stunned me into silence. However, while I may have been at a loss for words, rage filled my body. I was shaking like a leaf, but I didn't bat an eye. Instead, I calmly took a deep breath and turned my attention to the children, while my classroom aide, Michelle, escorted Inaam to the headmaster's office.

It was then, in the eyes of my students, that I regained my balance and redirected my energy to these children who so desperately needed the consistency and continuity that only school could provide in their lives. Watching the Muslim children sitting together in the block corner during imaginative play, reenacting the planes knocking down the towers, I knew I had to use all my inner strength to redirect them in a positive manner. I had to make this moment a teachable one. So immediately I set to the task of going on with the lessons of the day, thinking that things could only get better as a result. I learned, though, after Michelle returned to the room, that my day was to be full of challenges.

When we finally had a peaceful moment to talk, Michelle told me, "Inaam made quite the scene upstairs as she demanded that Ikram be removed from your class. She feels he shouldn't be taught by an American teacher."

"Pardon? Is she serious?"

Michelle shook her head. "Yes, she was certain. But the headmaster would have none of it and was adamant that Ikram remain in our class."

I had no idea what my headmaster's rationale was, but I had to go along with his decision. While I was both scared and enraged, I knew it was my duty as a teacher to give Ikram the same care and guidance as the other children. Although his mother's words were a personal attack, I knew the only way to prove to her that she was wrong was through my actions and not through my words.

So with many deep breaths, and reminding myself constantly how much I love to teach, I spent the rest of my school year working to do just that. I devoted myself to those children and spent endless hours making sure that each was given the tools he or she needed to be the best student possible. I immersed myself in their lives, learning about their various cultures and trying to connect to each one on some personal level. Since they were only four and five years old, it was easy to find common interests among everyone.

Storytelling became our means of communication and a common ground we all could share. It was through the pages of picture books, rich in illustrations and words, that the students learned about the world around them. They began to shift their play from the violence of destroying towers in the block corner to dressing up in housekeeping or "going to the store" on their tricycles at recess.

Unfortunately for some of my students, the language barrier was not always easily overcome. Ikram was one of those students. Since his mother was a constant presence in school, always keeping a watchful eye on my classroom, I decided to involve her so she could see things firsthand. This way, we could be on the same page and not feel so threatened by each other.

Ikram's first language was Bengali, and he was having a hard time understanding some of the English stories we were sharing in class. In an effort to make the playing field more even for Ikram, I asked his mother, fluent in both English and Bengali, to read some of the books on tape in Bengali so the Bengali-speaking children could enjoy the stories both at home and in school. At first, her response was very reserved, but as Inaam saw the positive effect it had on her son, things began to change. Slowly but surely, Inaam became more amicable.

Impressed by the way I had made the books more accessible to my non-English-speaking students, my headmaster asked me to host a springtime breakfast for the parents. The goal was to show them ways they could become involved in their child's schoolwork in both math and reading. Once again, I asked Inaam to help; this time, she accepted graciously, and together we ran a wonderfully successful session.

Somehow, by including Inaam rather than alienating her or ignoring her, I was able to show her that, indeed, her preconceived notions on the morning of September 12 had been wrong. As one school year ended and another began, I looped with my class. I had the same students as in year one, Ikram included. Sadly, due to unforeseen family circumstances, I was unable to complete the year with my students and had to return to the United States in the middle of the school year. My departure was bittersweet and brought an end to an important chapter in my life.

The morning of my last day at school began like any other, until I opened the door to my classroom. I was greeted by the families of my students wishing me well and thanking me for all I had done for their children. Inaam was off in the corner, aloof in her posture and mannerisms. As the crowd cleared and the bell rang to start the day, she approached me.

"May I have a word, please, miss?" she asked.

"Of course," I responded, hesitant but eager to hear what Inaam had to say.

"Thank you, miss." Her voice was strong and clear, just as strong and clear as on September 12, 2001. "Thank you for all you have done for my son."

"You are quite welcome. It has been my pleasure to work with Ikram." I went to shake her hand.

Yet rather than take my hand, Inaam embraced me. Then she paused and looked me in the eye. "I was wrong to think Ikram should not have you for a teacher. I was wrong about many things."

As she turned away, I was once again stunned into silence and tears filled my eyes. Before leaving the building, she turned around and waved, whispering words of thanks and blessing.

It was a moment that once again left me speechless and one I carry with me every day that I teach. For not only had I made a difference in the life of a child, I had made a difference in the life of his mother as well.

Now, eight years later, I can see that my experience with Inaam helped draw me into the world of the inclusion classroom. Having been the outsider in London, I have firsthand knowledge of how important it is to stay true to my beliefs while doing the best I can for each of my students. I have made it my mission to ensure that my classroom is a place where the children feel free to take risks, where fair is not always equal, and where everyone receives whatever tools they need to reach their potential. The results have been amazing for student and teacher alike.

As a teacher, I make a conscious decision to celebrate difference on a daily basis. However, it was not until my differences were put into question that I was able to see the importance of doing so. Although Inaam's original words will always stay with me, so too will her words of good-bye. For it was my response to her that has made me a better, stronger, and more compassionate teacher and person. It is truly amazing the power words have and the impact they can have on a person's life. However, it is how one reacts to these words that can make all the difference.

OH YES, HE CAN!

Johanna Chesser

EVERY NEW TEACHER has internal conflicts. I definitely had my fair share when starting out, and I still have them even though I am going into my fourth year of teaching. When I was asked last year to teach with a special-education inclusion teacher, Mrs. Baker, my first inclination was to say no. After all, I had enough issues teaching in a regular education setting, dealing with students who are from very poor homes where there is little or no stability, few fathers or male role models, no exposure to other cultures, and (to top it off) no real emphasis on education. I can recall taking these kids on a field trip to New Orleans: They were so excited to see things that you and I would consider ordinary, like eighteen-wheeler trucks and road construction on Interstate 10 and Lake Pontchartrain. We passed the Superdome, and one would

20

have thought these kids had seen one of the Seven Wonders of the World. They said, "Ms. Chesser, it's so big!" Just like little kids.

So I thought about it and decided to open my classroom to the inclusion teacher and the special education students. Besides, I thought, "Two teachers in the classroom are better than one, right?"

Instead of being negative and focusing on what could go wrong, I decided to concentrate on what could go right. After all, I had great chemistry with Mrs. Baker, and I'd always admired her because she did her job so well and had a ton of knowledge that could help me be a better teacher.

On the first day of school, I arrived early because I wanted to be there to greet every student and to meet the few parents who actually cared enough to bring their children to school on that special day. I was excited, had a positive vibe going, and was really ready to get the school year under way. I glanced down the hall, and that's when I saw him. His name was Glen. He was a kindergartner, and I would see him in the hall every day that year. He would always smile and speak to me, and I would tell him, "You'd better get ready for first grade!"

Glen's smile only got bigger, then he would walk away to continue with his day. I heard so many negative statements about him that I was instantly intrigued. It is so hard to ignore something once it sparks your curiosity, and this child certainly sparked mine. I really wanted to help him, and told myself, "This is why I decided to teach, after all."

I soon learned how developmentally delayed Glen was and that he couldn't make it out of kindergarten on his own. I remember being shocked when I was told that he couldn't even write his own name. This was hard to understand, as a teacher and as a person. Glen was a repeat kindergartner, and still this poor baby could not write his name. He was promoted to first grade, though, due to school policy. Glen was going on seven years old and was simply too old to be in a kindergarten classroom anymore. I assumed he would be placed in my classroom since I had the support of the special education teacher, but instead he was assigned to a different first-grade teacher, a young woman who was in her first year of teaching.

I knew Glen, and I remembered how hard it was to be a new teacher. So I asked to have him in my class. His original teacher, Ms. Shelly, was concerned, but I really felt that he would benefit from being in a classroom where his issues could be addressed directly. We had a meeting with the principal, and all agreed that Glen should be transferred into our class. Thus my journey with Glen began. After that meeting, I still had to wonder, "Can I help this child and have some kind of positive impact on him?"

As the teacher, I am supposed to have an open mind and always be ready to handle the unexpected. The first day Glen came into our classroom, my first thought was, "It can't be as bad as they say it is." We all tend to exaggerate just a little, but everything I'd heard about Glen was 100 percent accurate. This poor child was seven years old and clueless. He couldn't identify the alphabet, numbers, or color words. Glen couldn't hold a pencil, and he still could not write his name. That first night, I asked, "What have I gotten myself into?!"

Feelings of doubt and uncertainty filled my mind. It was obvious to me that this child should have been placed in an alternate learning environment where he could receive more one-on-one time, but paperwork and red tape and lack of parental involvement brought that process to a standstill. The decision-makers' hands were tied because changes like this couldn't be made without parental consent. Glen was a regular education student on paper, but the inclusion teacher decided to work with him as if he had an individualized education plan (IEP). Mrs. Baker treated him as if he were one of her special education students, and I gained even more respect for her. I was determined to help him but realized I still had nineteen other students in the classroom who needed my help. Most of them were not classified as special education students, but many were also behind in their academic development. "What a challenge!" I thought.

It is easy to take on the challenge, though, with students like Glen. So many people said he was the "can't do it" child. He had no positive male role model and a mother who would only curse and threaten to whip him as if it were his fault he couldn't perform in the classroom. He had a sister in the second grade who was angry because she had to take on the role of "mom" at home, even though she had her own schoolwork to attend to.

Because of all this and so much more, I was told I would never get Glen to write his name. I was told he would never do it no matter how hard I tried. I know one thing, though: I am the teacher, and I am supposed to face all obstacles. And that's why I refused to accept that a child in my classroom would never write his name.

Days passed, weeks passed, and the end of the first month of school was quickly approaching, but Glen was making no progress. I used a special font and typed his name in dots, so that all he had to do was trace the dots.

I asked Mrs. Baker, "How can you trace dots when you can't hold a pencil?"

"I don't know, Johanna," she said. "But we'll find out."

I believed in her, but on top of the difficulties he had with motor skills, Glen was not aware of the letters in his name, so he didn't even know why I had chosen those particular letters for him to trace. Mrs. Baker and I continued to sit next to Glen and guide his pencil hand. We then moved on to modeling, hoping he would simply repeat the action. We got nothing.

"Let's take a few steps back," Mrs. Baker suggested as we discussed Glen over lunch. So we did.

We went back to the basics and started with simple dots while holding his hand, then we made straight lines, then we made slanted lines. For a week or two, we did this with him, and eventually we made major progress. Glen was able to draw lines and dots without our assistance. We remembered to always reward him for his accomplishments, no matter how small.

It seemed, though, that the setbacks outweighed the gains, and major frustration came into play on both sides. Glen became defiant because he was simply overwhelmed. He thought drawing lines and dots was good enough, but we let him know this was not acceptable. The moment we put the paper on the table, he simply shut down.

"I am not doing this," I remember him saying. "And you cannot make me!"

I tried explaining to him why he had to learn how to write his name. I continued to use rewards, but they had lost their impact. I tried the soft, motherly voice and I tried the tough, intimidating voice. I even took away privileges like recess when he did not comply. Nothing. This went on for weeks and months, and needless to say I was beginning to think, "Here is one child I cannot reach." It brought me to tears. Some of my co-workers and friends did not understand why I cried, but to me it was simple: I am a teacher, and I am supposed to make a difference with every child who enters my classroom, no matter what odds are stacked against them. I cared, and I was not ready to give up on Glen. I knew I would feel like a failure if I didn't continue trying to help him. Winter break was approaching, and in a way I was happy because maybe we all needed time to clear our minds. I could tell that Glen really needed a break, but I was afraid; I knew that for the two weeks we were off, Glen would backtrack because no one at home was going to help him.

We returned to school, and I kept telling myself, "Don't give up. He will get it!" But just as I predicted,

Glen had lost ground. With that, I decided to go back to the dots to get him back on track. But I also decided that I needed to change my approach, since Glen wasn't going to change. I was the adult, and I knew better. I walked to his desk and said calmly, "Let's try this together."

When he looked at me, this time he saw a confident teacher instead of a frustrated teacher. I realized that perhaps I had been counting on Mrs. Baker to lead us when, in fact, it was my classroom and Glen was my student. He heard something different in my voice, so he cooperated. He allowed me to help him, and just like that we were back on track. Glen's confidence began to grow, and I saw him for what he was: a flower blooming in spring after a long, cold winter. My other students were doing advanced activities, but in his mind he was one of them because for the first time he was using a pencil without any assistance.

And eventually, Glen learned how to trace his name without our help.

Once he mastered tracing his name, it was time to move on to writing the letters. Glen could trace his name, but he couldn't spell it. So once again we had to backtrack. We did various activities to get him acquainted with the letters in his name: blocks, magnetic letters, wiki sticks. I also asked his sister and his friends to stop calling him by his nickname and to use his real name in order to help him learn it. Glen eventually learned the letters in his name, and now it was time for him to reach for the prize. It was time for him to write his name.

I placed the paper in front of him, this time with no dots. His name was at the top for guidance, and he simply needed to write it on his own. My honest thought was, "He's not ready for this." That was inside. On the outside, I showed him my most confident face. I gave him the paper and walked away to address the other students in class. Five minutes later, someone tapped me on the shoulder. I knew it was Glen before I even turned around, but I was reluctant to face him. I truly feared another defeat. But Glen was smiling, just like last year when I would see him in the hall, only bigger. His smile was so wide, I thought his mouth was going to stretch out to his ears! I took the paper from him and had to do a double take. I couldn't believe what I was seeing. Glen had finally written his name, his first name and his last name. It was something so simple for so many, but it meant the world to me and Mrs. Baker. And, of course, to Glen. After all the months and all the emotions and all the battles and all the set-backs, Glen had written that name.

He had done something most thought he would never do. We never gave up on Glen, but most important, Glen learned he could do something if he really tried. I truly believe that for the first time in his seven short years on this earth, he felt that people believed in him. It was an especially sweet moment when Glen's kindergarten teacher told him how impressed she was and how very proud she was of him.

This is what happens when a teacher believes in a student. We need to believe when no one else is there to believe for them. It's our duty to step in and play that role. Sometimes the smallest accomplishments can make the heart and soul feel wonderful. I truly believe that when students have no one else to be their cheerleader, teachers need to be there to cheer them on. "You can do it," we teachers tell them. "If you stay the course, you *will* succeed—whether it is writing your name or writing a term paper. I get asked all the time, "Why teach? You can do something so much better." I reply with this story, as it is the best way I know to answer the question.

WHEN DOGS CAN TALK

Lisa Santilly

AS A FIRST-TIME visitor to our classroom of deaf and hard of hearing students, you might assume that you will be entering a quiet, calm environment. Some children might be effortlessly communicating their thoughts and feelings through their artistic and visual language, while others will have their heads bowed, working quietly at their desks.

In reality, it is a Monday morning and I am sitting at my desk, enjoying my last few minutes of peace as I make some final notes for a lesson on English verbs that may end up not being used. During my short time teaching, I have learned that the students usually crave conversation in American Sign Language (ASL) after spending the weekend at home. Most of them come from families where no one else can sign, and the children's ideas, thoughts, and opinions are muted until they enter the playground at school. Giving the students a chance to express themselves in a social atmosphere is sometimes the greatest lesson plan I can create for them.

The morning bell rings. Usually my students are the last to join the lines, as they take their cue from the hearing students that school is about to begin. But not today! Before I can even see her, I hear Ming shrieking my name, "Eeee-ahhh!" My students call me by my first name, Lisa, as surnames are rarely used in a deaf classroom. She continues screaming as she runs through the door and signs, "Frog!" "Frog!" while her other hand is pointing at the door. Next, Reggie and Nenita run in behind her. I notice that Reggie is sporting new geometric cornrows that his mom fashioned for him, and Nenita is wearing a new party dress that is most likely a hand-me-down from her Filipino cousins in New York. They squeeze past Ming, signing, "Maria!" "Frog!" "Frog!" Each child is now vocalizing, all waving their hands in my face and tapping my shoulder for my attention. Nenita signs, "In her purse!" Next enters Charlie, slowly dragging his bag. He is not a morning person. He helps me put the pieces together. He signs, "Maria has something in her purse .... Wrong!" He shakes his head, imitating a disappointed parent.

While Ming, Reggie, and Nenita continue to shout, wave their hands, bang on my desk, and jump up and down, Maria casually walks in holding a Barbie purse close to her chest. She quietly hangs up her coat and bag and takes a seat at her desk. Then, not so discreetly, she buries the purse inside the desk. She takes out her hands, looks at me, and signs, "What?" When I ask her to show me what she has in her purse, she slowly pulls it out and opens it to reveal a small, frightened gecko that is barely alive. At the same time, everyone decides to give their own rendition of what happened in the playground, but we are interrupted by someone at the door flashing the overhead lights. We look up to see Mary, a teacher from the deaf and hard of hearing kindergarten class next door. Mary, who knows Maria as well as I do, suppresses a smile while signing to her, "Maria, your brother has phoned the office and says that you have something of his. What should I tell him?" Maria lifts her eyebrows and shrugs.

After we make arrangements for the gecko to get back home, I gather my class in our semicircle of desks (everyone can see the signer in this formation) to have a discussion. Apparently, Maria thought it might be a good idea to take her brother's pet to school. Unfortunately, the gecko took more than one tumble in the snow, which upset some of the children. Of course, we take this opportunity to teach the kids that the pet was not a frog but a type of lizard, while my educational assistant frantically searches the ASL database to find a sign for "gecko." Books are brought in from the library, and a site on geckos is brought up on the computer. So much for my lesson on English verbs!

My classroom is anything but silent or tranquil, and my students are the happiest, most excited, curious, and challenging group of kids I have ever met. Many of my curriculum-based lessons take a backseat to teachable moments like this one, as the student have large gaps in their learning and understanding of the world due to their deafness. There is also the fact that our school is in Toronto, a very multicultural city. In my classroom alone, we have first-generation children from the Philippines, China, Portugal, Ghana, Trinidad, and Mexico. I am a teacher of the deaf and hard of hearing, assigned to a congregated classroom within a regular school. Although the bulk of their learning takes place in my class, my students (accompanied by an ASL interpreter) have the chance to integrate into hearing classrooms for classes such as physical education and visual arts. Our lessons are taught in American Sign Language, signed English, and written English. At home, these children often learn to lip-read their family members in their own language, accompanied by homemade versions of sign language. More often than not, the newly immigrated families are trying to establish themselves in Canada, learning English, finding employment, and getting through paperwork. Unfortunately, learning ASL is not their top priority. At school, the children have taught me how to mouth endearing words so that the conversations make more sense to them. When talking about "Grandma" and "Grandpa," not one of my students uses the English phonetic mouth formation. Consequently, I have had to learn to mouth the correct language name when communicating with a particular student. When speaking to a group, I sign the word but don't move my mouth at all. This helps bridge the communication gap that is shared by all because of the class's diversity—including me. At home, things are not so easy for my students. Often, they are left out of important family discussions. The dinner table becomes a fighting zone as the deaf child grows agitated when he or she is not able to keep up with the conversations flying across the table. On many occasions, the parents have asked me to make sure their child understands what is going on at home, as concepts such as death, divorce, or moving are too complicated for the parents to convey. Seemingly simple concepts can also be difficult. This is something my five pupils in grade two taught me.

Maria, whose family had emigrated from Portugal, was a feisty girl who often resorted to showing her frustration through negative behavior. She could hardly communicate with her family. Maria spent quality time with her mother doing tactile activities like cooking and cleaning, during which more visual communication could be used. I was blessed with a Portuguese educational assistant who could interpret the Portuguese dishes Maria had made the night before and explain them to me. A favourite was a type of pork stew called *cozido à portuguesa*. She also loved desserts such as *pastel de nata*, which is a small custard tart sprinkled with cinnamon. Maria had two older brothers who tormented her by teasing her, hiding from her, and for the most part bullying her. She, in turn, did this to her classmates. Maria was bright, but because of the lack of communication at home she often struggled with primary concepts. At the beginning of grade two, after spending her eight-week summer holiday at home, she couldn't even remember how to spell her last name.

One morning as the children were chatting about their weekends, I saw out of the corner of my eye Maria signing to her friend about her aunt and her dog. Maria signed, "The dog asks my aunt for food and then my aunt will tell the dog to wait and she will get it." Maria signed that she had a hard time lip-reading the dog's words. It took me a minute to realize that this eight-year-old believed that dogs could talk like humans because of the interactions that she witnessed between animals and people. She saw her aunt say, "Walk?" and the dog respond by barking (which, in Maria's mind, was talking) before getting up to be leashed. I signed to her, "But dogs don't actually talk with words like other hearing people, right?" And Maria replied, "Yes, of course they do. That is why my aunt knows what the dog wants. I'm deaf. I can't hear what the dog says to my aunt!"

At that point, I became alarmed. "How many of my other students think this way?" I wondered. Of course, I had never taught anything pointedly about this, even though we had read books that contained words like "meow" and "woof."

As it turned out, two of my five grade-two students thought that animals, especially cats and dogs, could talk just like people. One student was unsure, and only two were positive they didn't. This teachable moment must have lasted another hour as I made sure that the students knew that dogs say only "woof" or some similar noise and that hearing people can tell by the intensity or the type of bark what the dog wants. I tried visually to represent all the different barks or meows that might be interpreted as a message. I then went through all the animals I could think of to make sure they understood. After this, I excused myself and went to tell Mary what I had discovered, and she, in turn, made sure that her students were aware of the communication differences between animals and humans.

As a hearing teacher of deaf students I learned that I need to be much more aware of how my students assimilate everyday visual information. Even though I think I am aware of and accommodate for these disparities, I couldn't have foreseen this revelation. What I consider common knowledge in my hearing world is not so obvious to children who are deaf and have little access to information within their own environment, especially at home. My students constantly change my life and challenge me to see the world through their eyes. Whether it be learning a new word or phrase in English or independently ordering their first meal at McDonald's, I feel so proud of them. I witness them overcoming some of the obstacles that they face on a day-to-day basis and hope that in some small way I have prepared them for the barriers and prejudice they will encounter throughout the rest of their lives.

THE STAR,
A HEART WITHIN

Patricia M. Castellone

I WORK IN A suburban district, predominantly wealthy and middle- to upper-class. Most parents are college-educated, and the children have a wide exposure to extracurricular activities, lessons, and sports. Currently, I am teaching a regular education third-grade class. I have twenty students, some with special needs and some unclassified but reading below grade-level. I have been a teacher for eight years and have my elementary education, special education, and reading literacy certifications.

This past year, I decided to focus on differences within my classroom. Diversity was a districtwide theme, one that I am an avid believer in supporting. It is important that my students be exposed to a wide variety of learning styles, personalities, cultural influences, ethnic backgrounds, and ability levels. I wove the theme of diversity into my curriculum in as many content areas as I could, and during our daily class read-aloud, I would specifically select a text related to a particular theme of diversity. Working through these stories with my students enabled me to model how, as a class, we would respectfully promote discussions about our reactions and thinking. Often our discussions would evolve into goals we might set as a class, or topics that we wanted to expand by bringing concepts home for family discussion. These at-home interactions frequently evolved into powerful writing responses and literacy-based artistic extensions in the classroom.

Our character education program in social studies was a perfect vehicle to discuss diversity around the world, responsibilities, and awareness in our communities. As educators, we know that there is no time to add "more" to the curriculum. By weaving the concepts of diversity into my existing lessons, I was able to maintain my core curriculum for the students but also thoroughly enhance the personal connections, deepen them, and make them that much more meaningful.

An added bonus to my infusion of diversity in our curriculum was the impact this had on one particular student. Blake was an extremely needy young boy. He had recently been identified by our special education committee as having multiple problems, including severe ADHD (attention deficit hyperactivity disorder). Although in agreement with this diagnosis, Blake's parents chose not to medicate him. The research on ADHD reveals many opinions on the value of medication. Whether to medicate is usually a subjective decision based on the many nuances of a student's profile. Blake also displayed symptoms of minor OCD (obsessive-compulsive disorder) and extreme anxiety—all of which made it difficult for him to learn and demonstrate comprehension in our classroom setting. ADHD can be a challenge to manage in a class of twenty students. Support from special education service providers is often the best way for the classroom teacher to develop particular strategies that will enable the student to become more successful. A child with ADHD often benefits from structured expectations, frequent breaks, repeated directions, and lots of individual attention to check for comprehension. On top of this, Blake needed assistance because of the complications associated with OCD, which would manifest itself in the classroom if our schedule changed unexpectedly, if lessons went longer than usual, and especially if one of his service providers was late.

One reason I so looked forward to the meetings held around Blake was that I could better learn how to work with him, which in turn would help me to work with my class as a whole. The class was patient with him, but they were only eight and nine years old. I wanted to be sensitive to Blake's needs, but I also needed to acknowledge and authenticate the needs of the class as a whole. We are a class, a team. We value and support one another, but that can be a difficult balance to achieve. We were faced with a situation that was difficult for all the children and for me as their teacher. I constantly questioned my practices to see how I could best address Blake's needs without compromising the sense of community in our classroom.

In my building, teachers can get help with students they have identified as being in need of support. This help comes via a committee called the Child Study Team (CST). Teachers follow a process of recommending students for review, and at these weekly CST meetings the resource teachers, psychologist, social worker, speech therapist, and assistant principal were of great assistance to me in developing a plan of action to best meet Blake's needs. The specialists meticulously explained each of his diagnoses to me and offered to help develop modifications that would enable him to become more successful in the classroom. Our resource room teacher, a special educator, advised me that "Blake needs a lot of assistance. You will need to check in with him throughout the day, during each lesson, and especially during transitions. He is at high risk for tantrums and screaming fits, and *will* bring much attention to himself and your class." This was further enhanced by our school psychologist, who helped me draw up a specific behavior intervention plan with a goal of strengthening Blake's feelings of self-worth.

Blake would often have outbursts and tantrums—some violent, others screaming and crying—but he was a student whom I loved and cherished. Early in the year, a particular outburst really illustrated his struggles. At the time, we had begun a new nonfiction writing and science unit on animals. The animal assignments for the unit were picked out of a basket, and the initial task was for the students to write two questions about their assigned animal. They would then share those questions with the class. Next, I would introduce the students to the research tools they could use to help find answers for their questions. Each day, the students were taken through the steps of researching, note taking, paragraphing, and illustrating their findings. The outcome of the unit was a class "question and answer" book about animals. On the first day of the unit, Blake was assigned a hyena. He had never heard of this animal, and that threw him for a major loop. He began interrupting me, calling out, and yelling for my attention. "Uh-oh, a meltdown is about to hit us," I thought.

"How am I supposed to do this?" he cried. "I've never heard of this animal, Ms. Castellone! I don't even know what it looks like. Where does it live? How am I supposed to do this? I can't do this. *Give me a different animal!*"

Blake was screaming and pulling at his hair. This was by far his worst outburst yet. I calmly pulled him aside and showed him the books I had on hyenas. Unfortunately, it didn't help. The other kids were now beginning to back away, returning to sit in their seats, as far away from Blake and me as they could get. I attempted to calm him by explaining that the purpose of the project was to be exposed to new animals and to learn a few new things. He looked at me, his eyes full of tears and his hands still pulling at his hair, but he was no longer screaming. He was still breathing hard, though, and I could tell that this wasn't over. Knowing that he enjoyed working on the computer, I sat him down to Google "hyenas." I showed him the connection between the African plains and the hyenas in Disney's *The Lion King.* As he navigated through the website, still breathing heavily and with one hand gripping his leg, I called the main office for some assistance. My students were frightened and staring. They weren't quite sure how to react, and I reminded them to carry on with their work.

The office secretary sent the social worker right away, and she sat with Blake at the computer. They talked about the importance of the assignment and how much fun it would be to learn about a new animal. Once he was calm, she removed Blake from the classroom and worked with him in her office. As time went on and the members of the CST continued their work with me, I became not only more confident in myself but also more aware of the small things that might trigger these behaviors. Over the course of these meetings about my struggling student, we created a plan using social stories and "I" messages for Blake to convey his feelings and emotions. There was a great deal of support available for Blake and me on a daily basis, and through this spiraling experience I truly learned a great deal about myself and the many ways that I can work to meet *all* my students' needs.

At the end of each day, Blake was never far from my thoughts. As I planned my lessons for the days ahead, I always considered how both the class and Blake would react. I would review my plans to try to predict what might trigger an outburst or excite him to a point where he could no longer be productive. As respectful as the class was, I knew that Blake caused much angst, both to me and to my students. They struggled to understand Blake, his neediness, his outbursts, and—perhaps most confusing, and definitely most disarming—the fact that he could be so irresistibly charming at times.

I read a multitude of stories to my students this past year, including *My House Has Stars* by Megan McDonald and *The Hundred Dresses* by Eleanor Estes, each of which had a significant focus on diversity and acceptance.

The Hundred Dresses focuses on the bullying of those who look different or have different cultures; while *My House Has Stars* takes place around the world, with children describing their homes and communities. We learn through each child about the different details of their homeland and, perhaps more important, that we all live under the same night sky full of stars. On that theme, I taught a lesson in which the main idea was that we are all different but every one of us has a heart. We all share similar feelings and emotions, such as love. This lesson gave me feedback to the remarkable responsiveness of my students to the differences in our classroom. Initially, I asked each student to bring in an apple. We had yellow, red, green, and brown apples. We had perfect apples, bruised apples, small apples, and large apples. Each apple had its own characteristics. I had my students examine their own apple, become friends with it, then return it to our communal group of apples. The next morning, their writing prompt was to recall attributes about their apple and to describe them in their writing journals. After doing so, the students were asked to go to the table where I had placed all of the apples and try to identify their own.

Some students were able to locate their apple immediately, while others were not. When we discussed the reasons for this, the students listed the characteristics that they remembered. I then cut each apple in half (widthwise) and showed the students that inside each apple, no matter the color, size, or shape, was a star (the seeds and core form the shape of a star). I then carried this idea over to us as students, teachers, and people in general—the individuals who make up our classroom community.

With all eyes glued on me, I expressed to the children, "Each one of us looks different, acts different, and sounds different. We have different families, friends, and living situations. Some of us have a lot of money, some of us are super-smart, some wear glasses, and some do not. But inside of each of us—"

And this is where Blake stole my heart. He practically jumped out of his seat when he cried, *"A heart, Ms. Castellone! Each of us has a heart and feelings, and that's the same for every single person!"*

On that day, my students' attitudes toward Blake changed. They learned that although his differences were more obvious than those of most students, everyone in our room was different in their own special way. They understood that everybody has a bad day every now and again, just like him. On that day, Blake taught us all that he recognized his differences but accepted them and accepted each of his classmates for who they were: children, each with his or her own heart. And feelings. And emotions. We all live under the same sky, stars, and moon. We are all different, yet one and the same.

DIAMONDS IN THE ROUGH

Susan DeMersseman, PhD

IN MY MANY YEARS as a school psychologist, I have come to see that diversity is much more than skin deep. As the clever fox explained to the Little Prince, "What is essential is invisible to the eye. It is the time you have wasted for your rose that makes your rose so important." And it is the time I have "wasted" that makes some of the students I have worked with so important to me. Time with these children reveals much, sometimes amusing, sometimes heartbreaking, and sometimes hopeful. Tina's story was one of the heartbreaking ones.

I waited at the door of her classroom and watched this first grader as she shuffled over to meet me for our weekly session. She could barely keep her tattered sneakers on, but they were better than the Mary Janes that had been pinching her feet the week before.

This was the third week of working with this child. Her best friend had been killed in a hit-and-run accident, and Tina was with her when it happened. The caseload of a psychologist in a large urban school district has a mix of distressing cases. At that time, Tina's was the saddest. She was seven years old, saw her friend hit by a speeding car, and knelt beside her as she died. It was a terrible trauma, but Tina seemed to be handling it amazingly well. At school we tried to provide the best support we could, and my weekly visits were part of it.

On the day of that visit, Tina seemed unusually upset but I was unprepared to hear why.

"My mom's friend's staying with us, and her boyfriend came with a gun and shot holes in the walls and I tried to climb up on the shelf in the closet to hide." Tina went on to explain how she had tried frantically to climb up on that shelf but couldn't quite reach it. Quickly, our talk became one of the strangest conversations I've ever had with a child. We talked about the best place to hide when someone comes into your home with a gun. We talked about the benefits of being down low where bullets might be less likely to fly; about where you could run more easily if you needed to.

It wasn't until Tina left my office that I realized the weight of the encounter. Did I really just counsel a child about where to hide when someone is shooting a gun in her home? I was trained to help children talk about feelings and thoughts, but the reality was that sometimes we needed to talk about where to hide. It was sad, it was surreal, but it was necessary.

We knew at school that Tina's family situation was not good. The teacher suspected parental drug use, the neighborhood was tough, and Tina didn't appear well cared for. Her hair was never combed. Her clothes fit poorly and were seldom warm enough. She was one of many in this school with similar challenges.

At the time, my daughter was a few sizes ahead of Tina and growing fast, so the teacher asked her mother if it would be okay to share some things with her. When I took off the sneakers that were curling up her toes, it was almost a bigger relief for me than for Tina. I was near tears as I watched her run off to recess, bouncing happily in shoes that caused her no pain.

One chilly winter day, I brought a near-new jacket for her. It was bright green and puffy, with a cozy flannel lining. I will never forget her face as she took off her thin cotton sweater and pulled on the green jacket. She wrapped her arms all the way around as if giving herself a big hug. Tina closed her eyes and savored the warmth. To me, it was as if the jacket were doing for her what I wished I could do, giving her a place of comfort and safety.

Tina left school the next month. We heard that her mother was kicked out of the apartment and went to stay with friends in a nearby city. I didn't track her down. My caseload filled with the next set of crises, but I've never forgotten Tina. When I think of her, I try to picture her safe and warm in the green jacket, but even after many years I am haunted by an image of her terrified and trying to climb up on that shelf in the closet.

Whether from national or personal trauma, children in every corner of the world must think about the best place to hide. Our country is busy worrying about how to "leave no child behind" academically. But for Tina and for too many other children, concerns about phonics and feelings are luxuries they don't have.

Most of the cases are not so dramatic. Instead, there are the everyday challenges of scoring tests and writing reports, dealing with difficult parents, and giving advice to teachers who have run out of tricks and out of patience. I must also work with children who are so angry and oppositional that they seem beyond repair. But one part of my job, for which I'm most grateful, is the opportunity to find the glowing, valuable side of a child and show it to the rest of the world. Sometimes I'm able to dust off these little gems so that others can see the potential and nurture it with new hope.

Another wonderful part of my job is seeing the power of a few minutes of respect and tenderness. Many of the youngsters referred to me for testing are tough little boys, most of whom prefer to misbehave rather than look stupid in front of their classmates. For the purposes of my work, I need them at their best, to comply with the assessment and provide a "valid measure of functioning." But for the purposes of my heart, I want them to leave the short time we have together having experienced, and benefited from, respect and encouragement.

One such experience took place with Darren, a skinny, hyper little second grader. He was absent on the day I came to test him for possible learning disabilities. The school was determined to get him assessed, so the social worker called Darren's home and then went to pick him up. His mother had overslept. She was not a terrible parent, but the family was often in a state of some kind of chaos. She had lost four of her six children to the foster care system a few years before and was still trying to pull things together after getting them back. According to the school social worker, neglect and drug use had resulted in their removal; and now that they were back in the home, truancy had become a real problem.

Darren hadn't eaten, so we made small talk as he dove into the school breakfast. It is common practice to test in the morning and to never do so on an empty stomach. As we chatted, I helped him open containers. At one point, he paused and said, "Thank you." Not a remarkable response in some communities, but in this one it wasn't the norm. After helping him with a sticky syrup container, he offered me some of his waffle. I said, "No, thank you," and then, "You have such nice manners." He took a sip of his orange juice, looked up at me, and said, "You have nice manners, too." In such a chaotic little life, to Darren this slow, respectful encounter was worth noting.

On another day, I was asked to test a disruptive fourth grader, a big, husky boy named Richard. The school was

concerned more about his behavior than his learning disabilities, and my work was part of the process. I gave him
my usual explanation: "This is a test that will help us find
out what things you are good at and what things you need
help on. You can't fail it, but it will just help us know how
we can teach you better." I made it clear that some items
would be too hard and some very easy, and that I would
be happy to answer any questions.

Richard seemed quite engaged in the explanation, and
it was clear from the beginning that he had some wonderful potential. As we went through the testing, I stopped
to note (and encourage) such behaviors as persistence and
talking himself through the tougher items. As we pro-
ceeded, he seemed even more engaged in the tasks and
pleased with the positive feedback. The normal setting of a
large class and his behavior made positive feedback a rare
thing for him.

When we finished testing, I asked him what things
got him in trouble in class. He responded easily, "Talking
when the teacher is talking." I knew he tended to stir it
up with his classmates, sometimes even in physical confrontations. I also knew that his classmates liked to push
his buttons. Richard's goal was to be a football player,
so we talked a little about how football players are usually recruited by college teams. I reminded him of all his
potential and said that to get to college there were some
steps he might want to take right now.

I gave him a few visual metaphors to hold onto,
hoping these would help him to avoid distractions and

the kinds of behaviors that would keep him away from achieving his goal. He liked the image of "Don't take the bait." It helped him see that each time he swam past those who were trying to set him up, he had won. He needed to win sometimes, and this way could only help him. He also liked the idea of "flying below the radar" of cranky teachers. For someone who often called attention to himself in negative ways, this was another image he could hold onto and hopefully learn from.

When it was time to go, I said good-bye and started to put materials back in the test kit. In a completely spontaneous move, he bent over and hugged me before getting up to leave. I have no illusions. There was nothing so special about me that inspired the hug. It was that I made *him* feel special and valuable. I was a mirror that reflected an image that made him proud and hopeful about himself. Sometimes my job is to polish up these diamonds in the rough, not so that others may see their value but so that they can see their *own* value.

There are many communities in our country filled with Darrens and Richards. I also know that there are many people like me in those communities, grateful that our work allows us to look for what is good and unique in children and to shine a hopeful light in their direction—to offer them the comfort of a warm coat, help with a messy breakfast, or just a kind, encouraging word.

⊞

THE NAIL THAT STICKS UP GETS HAMMERED DOWN

Susan Laughlin

I HAVE JUST BEGUN my seventeenth year of teaching and have had the privilege of teaching on two continents, in three different countries, and in four of the fifty United States. I have observed many differences in learners, learning, and teaching styles, and this has made me the teacher I am today.

My career began east of Los Angeles in a largely Latino community that had its share of drug and gang issues. This community is located at the foot of the San Bernardino Mountains, about sixty miles from Los Angeles. During morning meeting, it was shocking to have a third grader talk about a drug bust he'd witnessed in his living room the night before.

This forced me to reflect on the best way to respond to "My daddy got busted for cocaine last night." It was what I had to do as this little boy's teacher.

His name was Hector, and I recall something else I learned from working with him and his classmates. One day during the first week of school, Hector and a friend were caught running from one room to another. Both averted their eyes while I spoke to them about it.

"Hector, Juan, *look* at me when I'm speaking to you! I expect you to be polite and respectful when I'm talking to you!"

A colleague explained to me later that I was in a position of authority; thus, to look me in the eye would have been disrespectful.

"A lot of these kids get reprimanded if they make eye contact," she said.

Just as shocking was the time I was body-slammed into a filing cabinet by a third-grade boy named Pablo. In hindsight, my blanket expectations for the class were well beyond Pablo's learning level. I required him to complete the same assignments as everyone else, even though I'd already noticed some of the classic symptoms of a learning disability. One day, Pablo had had enough of me hounding him for his homework, so he "jacked me up," lifting me off the floor and shoving me against a filing cabinet. I was shaken physically, but what shook me most was realizing how inexperience had led me to shortchange a student just because I felt it wasn't fair to teach him under a different set of rules and expectations. Fair does not always mean the same.

Gianna, another student I taught while in this school, exemplified the passion for learning that many of the kids had. Gianna was a happy little girl and a good student, so imagine my surprise when she asked me, "Did you ever visit your daddy in jail?" Nothing in my teacher training had prepared me for such a question, but I had to answer it with feeling. I said no and then asked her some questions about her father, focusing on the positive things she knew and remembered about him.

As usual, Gianna skipped out of my room, a resilient smile on her face. I had come to understand how important it is to connect with the whole child, from understanding his or her cultural background to accommodating weaknesses while capitalizing on strengths. When I looked at the world outside the four walls of my classroom, it was easier to see why Pablo hadn't completed his homework, or why Gianna hadn't come to school the day before, or why it was almost physically impossible for Hector to make eye contact with me when being scolded.

My first year of teaching, I consistently logged seventy- to eighty-hour work weeks and I still wasn't prepared for what each day held. I was devoted to planning detailed lessons and creating an environment that highlighted the achievements of each student. What money I didn't spend on rent and car payments, I spent on school supplies. It took me a long time to figure out that as hard as I might try to make things "right" in the world of my students, I couldn't change the circumstances of their lives. I needed to focus on what I *could* do rather than trying to erase the pain that infiltrated their childhood.

I taught in San Francisco for a few years and then continued west to Japan. My jobs included teaching English conversation to everybody from preschoolers to university students and adults. I gave private lessons and taught in community centers, and two common threads I noticed in my Japanese learners were humility and perseverance. They always understood more than they let on. One strategy I employed to teach conversational English while also connecting with my shy Japanese students was to use pop culture and entertainment. One movie that was quite popular with the college students was *La Bamba* (the story of the short life of 1950s singer Richie Valens). I think it appealed to them because of the music, the toughness of the characters, and the raw emotion conveyed in the film. Another pop icon who received heaps of attention was Michael Jackson. I remember Keiichi requesting a lesson. "Susan-san, can you tell me the words to Michael Jackson song?" This turned out to be a common request, so I took that lesson a step further and brought my university students to karaoke to sing Michael Jackson songs.

I had numerous discussions with a high-achieving group of students from Kyushu University about how the communication style in Japan is so different from that in the United States. We talked about how in the States, people come right out and say what they are thinking; how it is okay to share political opinions and the like. In Japan, it's much more socially acceptable to not share opinions, especially if they differ from those of a person who is older than you or has a more senior position in society. It all tied into a Japanese expression used to describe those who are different: "The nail that sticks up gets hammered down." Quite different from the emphasis we put on individuality in Western culture.

I had one adult student who finally gained enough conversational English to share her deepest secret with me. Feeling some sense of security in the fact that she wasn't speaking in her native tongue, Atsuko told me that her husband was having an affair. She was petrified of anyone knowing because of the shame *she* would bring to her family. I was outraged at the thought that her husband's actions could cause Atsuko to be shamed. Because of his choices, she couldn't speak out, lest she risk being "hammered down." She also had to consider her two young sons. Atsuko was willing to endure prolonged and intense mental pain in the name of saving face.

As horrible as her circumstances were, it was refreshing to hear someone share so openly and honestly. In the Japanese culture, there is *honne,* which means "inside face," and there is *tattemae,* which means "outside face." Some *gaijin,* or foreigners, believe that no matter how long you know a Japanese person, you will see only the outside face. Through the acquisition of language, Atsuko felt free enough to show me her *honne.* This was one of my most empowering moments as a teacher.

I taught English to two families, both of which I got to know very well. The Tanakas had three children, Akiko, Masanori, and Daisuke, and each Saturday night I would ride my bike to their house. After the lesson had been completed, I would go to the kitchen and be treated to traditional Japanese delicacies prepared by Mrs. Tanaka. Both parents, and sometimes the grandparents, would join this festive gathering, and we communicated through the children, who happily translated for each of us; what I couldn't communicate in my limited Japanese, and what the parents couldn't say in their limited English, the kids could say for us. I attended Akiko's *shamisen* (a three-stringed, lute-like Japanese instrument) concerts, was dressed in a kimono to celebrate Girls' Day, and was honored with a homemade mosaic sign made by the children in celebration of my upcoming wedding. My husband and I put the sign on the car after our ceremony. The teacher even became the student when Mr. Tanaka tried to teach me about humility: "Even if you're right, when you are in public, you let your husband be right. When you are in your house, you are the boss; but in public, he is the boss." Rather than judge Mr. Tanaka, I tried to see the wisdom in his comment. It was too hard to stomach, though, especially given the glimpses of oppression to which I'd been privy.

With an understanding of cultural differences, I have maintained a friendship with Mr. Tanaka and his family for more than twelve years now, ever since I returned to the States from Japan. Reflecting on my time there, I learned about respect, honor, and—yes, I will admit it—how to hold my tongue! This has helped me immensely in my teaching, and I carry something from each of the places I have taught every time I enter my classroom.

When I first returned to the United States, I taught at an elementary school just south of Madison, Wisconsin. Here, I experienced teamwork like nowhere else in my career. I worked with three fantastic teachers in a town with a strong Norwegian history. At different points, I had the opportunity to wear traditional Norwegian dress, hold a smorgasbord, and sing the Norwegian national anthem on Norwegian Independence Day. The honest style of communication among students, teachers, administration, and parents was quite a contrast to Japan and even to the Hispanic culture in California. My team leader, a dedicated professional named Lynn, was an outstanding model of "leading by example." I was hired to teach third grade four days before the school year began, on the Friday before Labor Day weekend. That night, Lynn called to say that she would pick me up on Saturday morning to go to the teacher supply store.

"We'll make sure you start the year on the same page as all the other third-grade teachers," she said matter-of-factly.

It was on this shopping trip that we discovered our shared allegiance to the New York Yankees (the 2009 World Series champs!), and our bond remains all these years later. Despite the fact that it was a holiday weekend, she didn't hesitate to help me. Her willingness to give led me to joke that my husband and I had come home to "the Japan of the States" by ending up in the Midwest. I will forever follow Lynn's example of selflessness whenever a new teacher comes on board.

Eventually I returned to my home state of Connecticut, and for the past four years I have taught language arts and social studies in New Haven at a magnet middle school for the arts. Some of the diversity I experience here is related to learning level and style. The first three years, I team-taught with a special education teacher and learned a lot about differentiating instruction—this despite the fact that she referred to my team as "those stinkin' Yankees"! We still say that we went through enough with our students to write a book of our own. This year I am learning even more about cultural diversity, as I have kids from Puerto Rico, Guyana, Trinidad, Malaysia, the Philippines, and the Dominican Republic. I strive to create an environment where students can celebrate their heritage by incorporating their diverse knowledge and experiences into our lessons. One thing we did early in the school year was create a "patchwork quilt" for students to display items, drawings, photos, and words that tell about their family, what's important to them, and where they want to go in life. Having worked with so many different kids in so many different places, I knew that an activity like this would be a great way to connect with my students right off the bat. It was also a great way for them to learn about one another. In the role of teacher, I find myself leading way too often. I'm striving to put the students in the driver's seat more and more every day.

Just last week, my class earned their first "blue slip party." This is a reward that the kids work on earning collectively for academic and behavioral triumphs. One thing they really enjoy about the blue slip party is that they get to decide what type of party we will have. Each morning, I have students from previous years stop in to say hello, get a hug, talk about what's up in their lives, or just look around to see what is the same and what is different from the year before. I told Darnell, a particularly tough student from two years ago, that our class was having its first blue slip party. He said, "Already? Wow, they must be good kids! They earned their first party way before our class did!" I reminded him that his class took a little longer to get going but that we celebrated many achievements his year as well. His comment made me reflect on how I continue to grow as an educator. Am I stricter? More lenient? More human? I don't know! Maybe a combination of all of the above? I'm not sure that ten years ago, five years ago, or even two years ago, I would have danced the way I did at the Michael Jackson dance party we had last week.

From the time my teaching career began in 1989 to now, my teaching style has changed greatly. I've learned how to meet children where they are and to use their learning level as a starting point rather than worrying about where they are supposed to be agewise or gradewise. I also know that each student is somebody's precious baby. I will be firm when I need to be, but I will also try to be fair in my expectations. I will follow through with everything I tell my students, as that is the least I can do. It is an important trait to model for them. I must lead by example! I don't think I really understood any of this as a beginning teacher, but I know I understand it now, especially after having two precious babies of my own.

Although there are many differences, there are also many commonalities in the places I have taught. Regardless of age, ethnicity, economic background, learning level, or home environment, all kids have a desire to achieve. No matter how hard their exterior shell may be, no matter the *tattemae* they show the world on a daily basis, within each child is an incredible young person just waiting to be molded, just wanting to learn, just hoping to share all the wonder that is stored inside.

Something's Gotta Give

Anne Dandridge Conrad

Becky was a biracial student who commanded much attention from her peers and her teacher. Any type of attention, good or bad.

For instance, one day when she was supposed to be working at her desk, I heard Daniel, another student, call out, "Hey, Mrs. Conrad! Becky is standing up in her seat swiping at your hanging posters with your pointer thingy!" I turned around in time to see her jump down and stand beside her seat, smiling coyly at me.

"Becky, what should you be doing right now?" I asked.

"Reading my story," she answered. By now, her head was hanging down and her bottom lip was sticking out in a pout.

"Okay, Beck, pull a card. You have lost five minutes of recess."

Angrily, she stalked up to the class chart and changed her green card ("all is good") to a yellow card (five-minute recess loss) and glared at me as she returned to her seat. Four days a week, the children would have either a written reading assignment or a math assignment. Most days, I could count on Becky coming in empty-handed and, in a baby-talk voice, answering, "I dunno," when asked, "Where is your homework?"

Walking down the hall to the cafeteria, library, or gym was a challenge for Becky. It seemed to be a skill she had bypassed in favor of running, hopping, or skipping to whatever destination she had in the building. "Becky, slow down, please!"

"Yes, ma'am!" she would yell as she continued to careen down the hall.

Taking away recess, sending her to the office, or even giving a lunch detention was a futile effort, as it never seemed to have an impact on Becky and her impulsive behaviors, not to mention her nonperformance in the classroom and with homework. In fact, she seemed to fight back even harder. Something had to change.

To get Becky to change, I had to change what I was doing. So I began to talk with her one on one. I sat Becky down across from me, and with her hands in mine, I said, "Becky, I know you are here. I can see you, I can hear you, and I am glad you are here." She smiled. "But you have seventeen classmates who deserve my attention, too."

From that day on, we talked a lot, just the two of us, and Becky began to trust me.

Learning about Becky's home life led me to the conclusion that these behaviors were definitely intended to draw my attention. Becky told me how her younger brothers were always into her things. And many times, her schoolwork was taken from her by her brothers. She told me there was a lot of loud talking because her brothers were impulsive and reckless. They commanded a lot of their mother's attention. I got the feeling that Becky was pretty much left on her own as the eldest of the four children. Becky's home was a two-bedroom trailer with three younger brothers, her mother, and her mother's current live-in companion. Her mother had two other children living out of state because she had lost custody of them. Eight-year-old Becky shared a room with her brothers, ages seven, five, and three. There was no washer or dryer in the trailer, so many times Becky and her two school-age siblings came to school in dirty clothes. The previous year, while in kindergarten, Becky's younger brother had a lot of behavioral problems and was finally suspended the last week of school for throwing a desk and hitting a classmate. The rumors were that the brother still at home displayed behavioral problems as well and would be an even greater challenge than the brother in kindergarten. Our home-school coordinator, Jackie, spent quite a bit of time talking to Becky's mom about parenting and how she could support her children at home.

Communication between school and home is very

important to me, so I gave parents my home phone in case they needed to contact me after school hours. When I told Becky's mother about Becky having lunch detention with me or with the principal, she punished Becky at home as well. Her punishments were never a teaching experience, and they hurt Becky emotionally. It was always taking something from Becky ... never giving her an incentive to work toward something, to promote good behavior. I stopped communicating with the mother concerning behavioral problems because the consequences at home were more damaging than supportive.

I asked all the parents to check over homework before signing their child's nightly assignment book. I sent home study guides a week before a unit test and encouraged parents to study along with their children. Parents who take an active role in their child's schoolwork have a very positive effect on the child's learning. From the beginning, I realized that interest in Becky's schoolwork was not a priority for Becky's mom, and certainly not for the adult male in the household. In fact, he told the teacher of one of the younger siblings to stop sending homework. Becky's mother would not sign the assignment book, so Becky did not do her homework. She would not help Becky study for a test, so Becky did not study.

"It's your recess you will lose, not mine, if you don't do your homework," the mother would say to Becky. The attitude at home was that homework belonged to Becky, and if she did not do it, then whatever school consequences Becky received was Becky's fault.

"But Mrs. Conrad said parents should study with us," Becky would argue. Her mother ignored her pleas, so I knew that someone had to give Becky the support that she was not going to get at home. While working with Becky in the classroom, I realized that she had a lot of potential and that with support she could be a good student. I also talked with her about accepting responsibility for doing her work even when others didn't help her; that there would be times in her life when the only person she could depend on was herself.

So at the end of the day, I began to carve out time for her to begin her homework. She also started going home on certain afternoons with a friend whose mother encouraged her and gave her time to do schoolwork. She joined the school-sponsored Girl Scouts group as well, after Jackie convinced her mom that this would be good for Becky. I tutored Becky, along with four other students, after school to prepare her for the state standards test. This was not easy, as the test covered work in the content areas going all the way back to kindergarten. She received extra help two days a week from our school literacy specialist and another tutor in reading. Becky had a lot of holes in her instruction due to the lack of support at home and her behavior at school. Even after this intervention period was over in late April, I wrote a note in Becky's assignment book and asked her mom to allow Becky to stay after school with me twice a week to continue her tutoring. I even offered to bring her home, but her mother said she would pick her up since their house was out of my way. So we continued to study for the standards test and also get homework completed.

During this time, Becky's behavior improved in school as well. Every day she would come in with a smile on her face and a hug for me. She became my little police person with the other kids. I had one student who never thought about how his words might affect others. Daniel was very judgmental of his classmates, always sticking his foot in his mouth and zinging the other kids with put-downs. He called them "stupid" and "jerkhead," and as far as he was concerned, what he said was okay because the way he saw it, "It's the truth!"

One day, Daniel said something cutting to another student and the class waited to see what I would do. Before I could say anything, Becky spoke up.

"Daniel, was that really an appropriate thing to say? I think you should apologize."

Well, if that wasn't the pot calling the kettle black! Becky had been just as impulsive with her mouth as she was in her physical actions and could zing put-downs with the best of them. Not anymore, though.

The class was quiet for a moment and then chimed in behind Becky's reprimand.

"Yeah, Daniel. That was mean," one child said.

"That wasn't very nice," said another.

"How would you like it if I called you that?" asked a third.

Daniel was speechless. For the first time, the class stood up and said, *"No more!"* All I could think was, "My job here is done!" Thanks to Becky.

I was just as proud of her work ethic as we studied together. She worked so hard and was so into wanting to learn more. I am proud to say that Becky's effort paid off and she passed all four standards tests. In the mornings when she gave me a hug, she would say, "You are the best teacher ever!"

And I would reply, "You are working so hard, and I am proud of you!"

A few days after the state standards scores were sent home, Becky's mother was in the front office to register the youngest brother for the Bright Stars program. Jackie was there, too, and happy to hear her talking about Becky passing all of her tests. When I saw Jackie later that day, she said, "Boy, Mrs. Conrad, your ears must have been burning earlier this morning!" I looked at her blankly, as I didn't know what she was talking about. "Becky's mom was here this morning, and she was so proud of Becky's scores on the Standards of Learning (SOL) tests."

"Oh, so you heard about Becky," I said, smiling. "I am sooo proud of her. You should have seen how serious she was during after-school tutoring sessions!"

I remembered how focused Becky was during online tutoring lessons. There was none of the playing around for which she was known. It was total "taking care of business" with her. We would finish a problem, and she would say, "Come on, let's do another one!"

Whenever her mother came to pick her up, Becky could not get the words out fast enough, telling her all that she had covered that day. Words were spilling over themselves as she shared the different subjects and skills we had reviewed together. She had all the enthusiasm of a great student, and I hoped that her upcoming teachers would see that. I certainly planned to enlighten them.

Standing in the office that spring day, Jackie added, "Becky's mom also said that she knew Becky could not have done as well as she did on the SOLs without your help, and that she knew you didn't have to do that."

At last! It sounded as if the light bulb had finally come on with Becky's mom. I will admit that, at first, I was angry at her for not giving Becky the support I asked for. I mentally accused her of being lazy and not accepting her responsibilities as a parent. I now realized that maybe Becky's mom didn't give the support because she didn't feel confident in her own abilities. I remember another teacher telling me, after she heard that I was spending extra days after school with Becky, that if it had been her, she would have said, "Well, if her mother doesn't care, then why should I?"

Becky made me see that my job as a teacher is to give as much as I can to each student. We cannot blame the child for the faults of the parent. Becky needed extra learning time. I could give that to her, and it was my responsibility as her teacher to do so. Becky deserved nothing less.

The Bodyguard

Shawna Messina

I BELIEVE TEACHING IS like the saying "Everything I learned, I learned in kindergarten," except the saying is more or less "Everything I learned, I learned my first year of teaching." A teacher will never forget her first class, she will always believe it to be her "worst," and it will be the first time she realizes that she *can* make a difference.

I had a disastrous start to my first year. I truly believed I was being railroaded by the principal, and my room felt more like a detention facility than a classroom. My room was filled with kids the other teachers had shrugged off as "problem" students. In my fourth-grade class, I had an alarmingly large boy—he was eleven, soon to be twelve, and he beat me in height and weight. Mark was a student who had previously "fallen through the cracks," and after only a few short weeks together, I realized Mark couldn't read.

Standardized reading test scores placed him in the thirtieth percentile, and he was reading fewer than forty words per minute. He basically looked like an eighteen-year-old but read like a first grader. It didn't take a genius to understand that Mark had behavioral problems not because he was a bad kid, but because he was avoiding the inevitable teasing.

In addition to the challenge of keeping Mark out of the principal's office, I had to provide reading instruction on his level without humiliating him. Without bruising Mark's ego, I was able to find material, usually from the first- and second-grade curricula, to modify my reading lessons for him. I placed him in a reading group of mostly girls because they were kind about his struggles and he didn't have to worry as much about protecting his reputation. He was driven by football, so I collected the sports pages, downloaded articles, and checked books out of the library for him. I love football myself, and I would watch the Dallas Cowboys game on Sunday so that on Monday morning Mark and I could review the highlights. He was unaware that by discussing the game, I was checking for his comprehension; he just enjoyed talking about football.

Mark was being raised by his father and stepmother. Thankfully, his mother, Mrs. Campbell, was aware of Mark's academic issues, and we met early in the year to discuss his behavior. She and I shared the same concern: How was Mark able to fool his previous teachers and not be held back in earlier grades with the reading comprehension and fluency of a first grader? After our first parent conference, I began to document his progress, keeping samples of his work, and I notified the school's diagnostician about Mark's academic deficits. The diagnostician gave me a detailed STEPS (Student Tiered Educational Plan) intervention plan packet that was an inch thick, and said that I would have to fill it out and provide Mark with six weeks of documented intervention before he could be considered for special-education testing. I reviewed the packet and quickly began to understand how Mark had "fallen through the cracks" in previous years: The paperwork was tedious and repetitious, and if Mark moved during the STEPS process, it would start over again at his new school. With all of that in mind, I started STEPS anyway.

Mark had been sent to the office during the beginning of the year because of a fight on the bus, and he was seeing the counselor to learn to control his temper. I had a couple of complaints from female students that Mark was bothering them at recess and during PE. Unfortunately, he had a reputation in my building for being a "bad" student, and it seemed the only place he *didn't* get in trouble was in the safety of my classroom. Students often make choices that are out of their teacher's hands, and Mark made the mistake of holding a girl down and putting his hand up her skirt. He had exercised this bad judgment on the school bus, and before the school day started, Mark was seated in the blue chairs outside the assistant principal's door. I was checking my school mailbox and was upset to see him sitting there so early in the morning. His face betrayed immediate shame.

"What happened, Mark? Did you do something wrong?"

His voice cracked and he could not bring himself to tell me what offense he had committed. My assistant principal gave me the bus infraction to read, and I was able to respond only with one question: "Why?"

He looked away, but I know he understood that I was very disappointed in him. I tried to hide my tears, knowing he wasn't going to get a pass back to class. For committing sexual harassment, Mark was sent to an alternative school for thirty instructional days, and I worried that the gradual progress he had made would quickly diminish. I also was angry to learn that the documentation I had been collecting on Mark would have to start over when he returned to my school.

The tone in my class changed. Mark's classmates and I missed his presence; he was an obvious leader in the room. I wanted Mark to know he was missed and we were anticipating his return. The students would write letters and draw pictures for Mark, and Mrs. Campbell helped us to keep communication open by playing mailman. I kept Mark's locker and desk the same, although I gained students while he was gone.

During Mark's absence, I received a new student named Jon, who appeared to have a real chip on his shoulder. I was told that I would have a meeting with administration, the counselor, and his mom, which worried me because that was not the usual policy for a new student. We met while Jon sat in the hallway, and I was informed we were having an ARD (Admission, Review, and Dismissal), which is a special education meeting. I wasn't sure what to say or how to behave, since this was my first ARD experience. Jon's IEP (individualized education plan) stated that he had been deprived of oxygen at birth and that he had learning and cognitive disabilities that placed his IQ in the range of a toddler. He had a behavioral plan, but it was just a basic outline of how to handle his immature behavior.

His mother made a plea for help in the meeting: "Can you please help me? My son is violent, and he set his sister's crib on fire last week."

I remember trying not to look appalled as I realized that this was going to be my new challenge. The committee decided to test Jon to see if he qualified as emotionally disturbed. In the meantime, I was to follow his IEP and behavioral plan.

Jon's first few weeks were difficult. He struggled with routines and was very aggressive toward the other students. I held his hand during the transition, and his desk was close to mine at all times. He thrived during recess, and although I had to watch the contact during the boys' flag football game, he began slowly to fit in. There were occasional outbursts, where he would curse or throw things, and he would exhibit bizarre behaviors for attention, such as blowing his nose and then eating the Kleenex. Every day was a struggle, but I did have hope that Jon was going to be successful and that he would make progress in my classroom.

I was pleasantly surprised when Mark returned motivated to learn. We gradually set goals for his behavior and grades, and with success Mark became even more of a positive leader in my classroom. I would tutor him before and after school, without the other students' knowledge, and Mark's confidence in reading grew. Mrs. Campbell and I began to develop a strong relationship, and she voiced her concerns again about Mark's reading level.

"I did try to have him tested at his previous school for special education. I'm pretty sure he's got a learning disability, the poor kid."

"I think so, too." Then I said, "What you need to do now is put your concerns in writing."

She followed through, and I turned in the completed paperwork to request he be evaluated. My frustration grew when I found out that it would take at least six more weeks to have him tested. I was beginning to feel that I had failed Mark, just like his previous teachers. I contacted Mrs. Campbell and told her that her voice was more important than mine, and she called the school weekly to see if Mark was being tested. With the two of us playing vocal advocates, Mark was finally tested. Eighteen weeks later, he was labeled learning disabled and would finally receive the services he so badly needed.

Just around the time I celebrated Mark's progress and success, Jon was labeled emotionally disturbed. Mark, who was the male leader in my classroom, tried to keep the peace and would volunteer to be Jon's partner or help him to read. Most of the time, I would work with both of them, but on this particular day I had a different small group. Mark was bigger than Jon, and for some reason, on this day Jon took Mark's presence as a threat.

"Stupid nigger!" he yelled.

Although Mark had been working on his temper, he was clearly upset. Then Jon pushed him, and my class erupted with the anticipation of a fight. I knew that if Mark fought he would again be sent to the alternative school, and I knew that Jon might not be able to control his anger and walk away. Without thinking, I got between the two students, and Jon threw me over a desk. The fall only hurt my pride. I was embarrassed because I landed on my back and my skirt flipped up. Mark picked me up and protected me until an administrator could come in and physically remove Jon. My principal wanted me to write a referral for Mark, saying that he was involved in the altercation, but I refused. Since Jon was older than ten, I had to make out a police report, and unfortunately Jon was sent to a juvenile detention facility. I praised Mark for protecting me, but it was a bittersweet feeling watching Jon taken away in a police car. I was happy to have witnessed Mark rise above his anger and become a positive leader, but I was also saddened to realize that I could not help Jon's situation or make a difference in his life.

I know teachers are not supposed to have favorites, but Mark earned a special place in my heart that year and I considered him my protector. I kept my part of the deal, and by the time our state standardized tests rolled around, Mark felt confident in his reading. With his classification as learning disabled he received certain accommodations, including being able to take the test at a lower reading level. I set the bar high, and Mark took the test on the third-grade level. It was all the help he needed, and he was able to pass his state test. Not only was Mark successful for the first time in reading, his reading level increased by two grade levels in one year. When I received the test results, I took Mark into the hallway.

"I've got good news! You passed your test!"

This child who looked more like an adult than a boy began to cry. He hugged me, which then made me cry.

"Mark," I said, "do you want your results to be our little secret? Or do you want me to share the news with the class?"

He said, "I would rather you tell them. Not my score, just that I passed!"

Obviously, he wanted to receive praise from his classmates, and that was just fine with me. I didn't want him to lose his reputation in the classroom as the tough guy, so I let him go to the restroom to get himself together. I announced his success when he returned, and the class began to cheer. That one moment made the entire year worth it, and I now hope for that moment each and every school year, the moment when you know that you made a difference. I have had many of these moments, but the first will always be the most memorable.

THE ELECTION OF 2008

Jeff Ballam

I KNEW THE CLASS would be special, but I would not know exactly how special until November of that year. I walked into that class with high expectations: high expectations for student learning and high expectations for fun in their learning as well as in my teaching. I had agreed to teach the class, a fourth-grade/fifth-grade split of all gifted students, and had prepared for it over the summer. In the era of No Child Left Behind, these students were indeed being left behind. They were being left behind in meeting their special needs, their need to excel, their need to be challenged, and their need to challenge. So I had planned my lessons around differentiating for the specific and distinct needs to push these students further in their academics.

After twenty-six years of teaching in the same school,

about ten miles northeast of downtown Los Angeles in a predominantly Hispanic neighborhood, I needed something different. I was burning out. In all those years of teaching I had had gifted students in my classes before, but never more than ten, and now I had twenty-six. Twenty-six for the whole day, twenty-six split between two curricula! The idea was daunting, but stimulating. I had a new direction for my teaching. Four years prior, I had taken on the role of gifted and talented education program coordinator in addition to my duties as a classroom teacher, and I had worked with many of the students in an after-school enrichment program the year before, when they were third- and fourth-grade students. So I knew many of them before the school year officially began.

The class was composed of eight fourth graders and eighteen fifth graders; ten girls and sixteen boys; one African-American female, one Filipino male, and twenty-four Hispanic students. I was the only Anglo in the room. The class was homogeneous as an entity in itself, yet quite diverse from the classes across the hall, from across the school, from across the country.

The first months of the year were living up to my expectations. Teaching the split was difficult, but we were managing. The fourth graders were independent and resourceful enough to guide one another when I had to focus on the fifth graders, and vice versa. We were given a scripted language arts program that suggested a five-day pacing plan per reading selection along with the accompanying lessons. We were breezing through in three. I added literature circles on top of the regular curriculum. The kids rose to the occasion. The class as a whole had a wonderful personality. They actually laughed at and *understood* my humor! Some could even respectfully dish it back. We had an excellent rapport. And they were takers. They took everything I had to teach and ran with it, thirsting for more.

But they also gave back. September is Hispanic Heritage Month, and it offered me my first glimpse of the deeper work of which these students were capable. I supplied them with a list of Hispanic leaders past and present, included a few historical events, and let them choose what to work on and how to present their work. Gifted students like the option of choice—choice of topic, choice of product. I was not displeased with the results: A beautiful poster board display of artist Frida Kahlo's life and work and a timeline of activist César Chávez and his struggles and successes in his work for the farmworkers were two of the projects that stood out. I saw for the first time what the effect of good differentiation could be. I received some of my students' best work in those products. I was fully prepared for a great academic year, but I was not prepared for what was to come.

November 2008 was a month of historic elections. Not only would the nation elect our first minority president or vice president, in California we would also be voting on Proposition 8, which would determine whether same-sex couples could legally marry in the state, even though an estimated eighteen thousand couples already had. My partner of thirteen years and I were one of them, and we were concerned for the fate of our union.

In the week leading to election day, I had taught my students about the two-party system and the candidate selection process for both national and state offices. We had discussed the historical importance surrounding the election, the first African-American presidential candidate of a major party and the first Republican ticket with a female vice presidential candidate. However, to avoid being accused of furthering "the homosexual agenda," I stayed away from discussing Proposition 8.

Election day dawned, a beautiful, crisp (for Los Angeles) fall morning. There was excitement in the air; it seemed both the students and the adults sensed that change and hope were on the horizon. I collected the class in the yard, and we walked upstairs into our room. I could hear the Obama chatter in the line. I thought I heard a couple of whispers surrounding Proposition 8. As we walked to our desks, Marlene, a fifth grader, glanced out the window and exclaimed, "They tagged the house across the street!"

As several other students ran over, I peered through the window and saw "Yes on Obama" and "No on 8" spray-painted on the house's front retaining wall. The pro-Obama graffiti drew praise, but the Proposition 8 message drew a mixed response. I suggested that instead of vandals, the owners themselves may have done it, as no other house had been so tagged. It made sense to the kids. And I wanted to get to the lessons of the day, which included a mock election.

But before we could get on with the work, Juana, a fifth grader never afraid of sharing her opinion, blurted out that it was wrong.

"What was wrong?" I asked, thinking she was still focused on the tagging.

"Not letting two people get married."

"You should be able to marry who you want," Rose piped up.

"That's just sick," commented one of the boys. "Two people of the same sex together."

"God says they're going to hell," Jeremy preached.

"Don't give me that!" Juana shot back.

I stood there, amazed at what I was hearing. I don't remember being that politically aware in fifth grade, let alone discussing something like gay rights. But back then, we didn't have something like Proposition 8 on the ballot. (Several years later, when I was in college, we would have Proposition 6, the Briggs Initiative, which prohibited homosexuals and their supporters from teaching. I remember my mother putting a "Yes on 6" sticker on our car.)

I finally settled the class down and into our mock election, which Democratic candidate Barack Obama won 25–1. The one lone student, a fourth grader, later said he had no idea who was who and just wrote down a name. I seized a teachable moment and pointed out the importance of studying the candidates and issues to know which way to vote.

Wednesday morning, with the results of the election all over the morning news, I collected the class. They were screaming, "Obama won!" but most were deflated that Proposition 8 passed. I tried to explain that the decision was still too close to call, and we would check in throughout the day. They became sensitive to the dilemma of those couples who had married before the law was changed. Juana was even distraught that all those couples might have to get divorced. Rose countermanded that making the couples divorce was unfair, as they had married in good faith under the law *at the time.* (These are ten- and eleven-year-olds!) I stood there, amazed at their insight. The discussion continued in the same vein for nearly a half-hour. I could not silence them. Many gifted students have an innate sense of justice. This election had set them off, and they needed to vent. I had no choice: I let them. Most students were in support of marriage equality, only a few were against it, and a smaller few, including all the fourth graders, were silent. As the day progressed and I informed my students of the proposition's status, they became more and more depressed over the potential outcome. Orlando, the class jock, ventured his opinion: "I think the 'No on 8' people should try again!" Others echoed his opinion.

Overwhelmed by their sensitivity and inspired by their optimism, as well as by Orlando's suggestion, I did some research on California's Proposition 22, passed by voters in March 2000, which also limited marriage to one man and one woman. I brought in the data comparing the results for both propositions: Proposition 22 (March 2000) 61.4 percent Yes to 38.6 percent No vs.

Proposition 8 (November 2008) 52.24 percent Yes to 47.76 percent No. I also shared with my students that in March 2000, only 37 percent of the eligible voters turned out to vote, while in November 2008, 59 percent of eligible voters actually voted.

I asked for the class' observations. The students were quick to see the difference. The trend was turning. Some students did question the effects of a March or November election in the outcome. We reviewed the differences between the primary and general elections, as well as a presidential election. They were looking at all the variables. The students devised a strategy: Wait for a general election in a presidential year to get more voters. But do try again.

Barely one week later, we began our statistics and graphing unit. Determined to have the students produce something more differentiated, I taught them the difference between an opinion poll and the ever-familiar "What is your favorite _____?" poll usually taught in the earlier grades. They were to choose partners and then select a topic. There were no limits on topic, except that it had to be something on which their respondents could share an opinion. They were to submit their choice of a topic by the end of the hour. Four of the teams had questions relating back to Proposition 8—they weren't letting it go! Two teams chose "Do you agree with Proposition 8?" and one team had a variant: "Was Proposition 8 fair?" Perhaps the most interesting, from Orlando and his partner, Gilbert, another jock, was, "Should the people against Proposition 8 try again?"

By now, I was concerned I would be accused of teaching "the homosexual agenda." I asked the class for their attention. I asked them who assigned their topic. They looked at me strangely.

"Did I assign you your poll topic?"

"No," many of them answered.

"So, I am not teaching you about same-sex marriage. Right?"

The understanding laughs and giggles told me I had nothing to worry about.

The summer before this class began, I had prepared myself by reviewing differentiation theories and practices. I had planned interesting and different lessons and projects, allowing students the choice of topic and product. I had acquired a variety of enrichment activities for those who finished early, thereby avoiding too much downtime. I had organized my plan book so that at times I would be giving direct instruction to one grade level while the other worked independently. I had prepared myself to let go of being "the sage on the stage," knowing there would be questions I might not be able to answer and to let that be okay, that we would discover the answer together. I had prepared for their academic success. What I had not planned on was a level of sophistication, compassion, and understanding usually associated with young adults.

In twenty-six years of teaching, I've learned that some of the best lessons are not in your plan book. They come upon you from out of nowhere, from the moment. And some of the best lessons come from the students themselves and are meant for the teacher.

I believe the future of my marriage, of the marriages of others, and of the country in general, is in good hands.

ANTHEM

Megan Highfill

"YOUR MISSION, IF you choose to accept it," I explained, giving each group a handful of folded paper strips, "is to put these phrases in order."

"You mean we have a choice?" Oscar asked, smiling deviously.

"No, no choice. I shouldn't have said 'choose,'" I answered, rolling my eyes at my dated sense of pop culture.

The students began unfolding the strips and reading them inquisitively, until some of them became annoyed.

"What is this word, 'per-i-lous'?" asked an eager girl sitting on the floor.

"How are we supposed to know this?" Oscar threw the strips on the floor and crossed his arms in protest.

"This is the national anthem of the United States of America." I sat next to Oscar and picked up his strips of paper. "It was written a long time ago, so it's a little hard to understand. Does anyone know the title?"

"Ooohh!" A girl raised her hand. "I know! I know!"

"Remind me of your name?" Seeing the students only once a week made it difficult for me to learn their names. Two months in, I felt as though I knew just half of our student population.

"Jessica. It's 'The Star-Spangled Banner'!" she exclaimed, satisfied.

"And the author, or the *lyricist,* as we say in music?" I looked at Jessica, and she dropped her head.

"Francis Scott Key," I told them. "He wrote the words and someone put it to the tune of an old British song."

I instructed them to complete the activity in their groups, and later we made corrections as a class.

"I still don't know what any of this means." Oscar shifted uncomfortably in his seat.

I could tell that Oscar's attitude was slipping quickly from his usual coping humor to a deeper sense of frustration.

At the risk of a class divide, I redirected the focus. "Stand up if the first language you ever learned in your life was English."

Nine or ten students stood, glancing nervously at the seated majority.

"Now, sit down if you have no earthly idea what these words mean." I wasn't sure if this would work. All but one student sat down.

"Jessica," I said under my breath. Now was not the time for a know-it-all.

She sat down as well.

"See, it doesn't really matter what languages you speak or where you are from. This song is difficult for everyone," I commented.

A few students nodded, but Oscar glared at the clock and seemed to be anticipating the bell. A few seconds passed, and the bell rang. He jumped up from his seat and jogged toward the door.

"Walking feet, fourth grade," I reminded the class. Walking up behind Oscar, I touched his shoulder. He ignored me. "See you next week, *bebés*," and I watched him leave without acknowledgment.

FRIDAY MORNING, TWO days after the disappointingly irrelevant national anthem lesson, I was reworking the plan in my office. The frustration had been visible not only in Oscar's class but in the other fourth-grade class as well. I hoped that the fifth grade would be more receptive, but I knew the order of activities needed work.

"We could talk about language at the beginning," I thought out loud. No, beginning with a lecture never works.

I tapped on my keyboard and waited for the desktop to load. There was a rough draft of a worksheet that might work for a starting activity, if my computer would ever start up. The worksheet required students to match the lyrics with a modernized sentence with the same meaning. "By the dawn's early light" became "As the sun came up." I was on the verge of cursing at my computer when I was startled by a soft voice.

"Missy ...," I heard from behind me. I spun my chair around to face Oscar, who dropped his coat and backpack to the floor and put his hands in his pockets.

"Miss Highfill," I corrected him. It was common for Spanish-speaking students to call teachers "missy" or "teacher," and though I didn't mind, I had been asked by my principal to remind them of the correct name.

"Miss Highfill," he continued, "I need to learn more of that song."

"What song?" I pulled over the band teacher's chair so he could sit down.

"That national song," Oscar replied, his voice rising in concern.

"Oh, yes." I uncrossed my arms, correcting a bad habit that my college professors said promoted confrontation. "The national anthem. 'The Star-Spangled Banner.'"

"I have to learn more of that song now." He stood and walked to the edge of my desk, helping himself to a stack of the cut-up phrases from the previous day's activity.

"We will learn more of that song, Oscar," I said reassuringly, taking the strips of paper from his hands. "We are all going to learn it. It's hard for everyone, remember."

"No, missy, I have to learn it *now*. And my mama wants to learn it, too. My whole family." He sat back down. "When they try to take me back, my mama says I need to know that song."

Though I considered myself eternally empathetic and full of diverse experiences, I could not comprehend what he was saying to me.

"But why now? And who is taking you where?" I asked him in Spanish, hoping that would break down some communication barriers.

He answered in English, "The police will take me. But if I know the song, I am American. My mama said that."

I leaned back in my chair and tried to avoid the internal political rant going through my head. Who made this child believe he would be taken away? Who told him he wasn't American?

When I didn't answer, Oscar pleaded with me in Spanish: *"Por favor, missy. Mi mamá me dijo que es importante."* ("Please Missy, My Mom told me that it is important")

"You mean, to become a citizen of the United States, you have to know 'The Star-Spangled Banner'?" I asked, shocked to be posing such an obvious question.

"Yes, that's it. A citizen." He seemed relieved that I finally understood.

"Are you sure you aren't a citizen already?" I felt overwhelmed, and hoped that, like many of my students, Oscar had been born in the United States after his family immigrated.

"I came here on the arms of my papa," he whispered, his eyes getting wide. He seemed unsure as to whether it was a good idea to reveal this information. He switched to Spanish: "I do not care if it is difficult. I have to learn that song."

After what seemed like several minutes of silence, I picked up his backpack and coat. "Go to class," I said as my first students entered the room. "I will come see you before the end of the day. Hurry, you'll be late."

Oscar left without looking back, and I wasn't sure if he trusted me anymore. I turned toward the chatty fifth-grade class, most of whom were sitting in their assigned seats.

"So ...," I exclaimed overexcitedly. "'The Star-Spangled Banner.'"

THE FIFTH-GRADE LESSON went as well as could be expected, considering my distracted mind and unedited modification of the fourth-grade lesson. The students seemed to understand the importance of the song, but the language was lost on them. I was pleased to be teaching at this school in Kansas City, Missouri, but felt too inexperienced to be teaching students as young as kindergarten and as old as eighth grade. Many of our students spoke very little English, and 100 percent of our population was on free and reduced-cost lunch. It was tough, but it was what I wanted, even if I felt out of place at this time. I paced the front of the classroom during the five-minute passing period. One more class and I could sit and think; cry, maybe. Though I had abandoned the theater in high school, teaching continued to test my acting skills on a daily basis. The next class moved in a quiet line into their seats, polar opposites of the previous set of students. Their pleasantly strict classroom teacher peeked around the corner at me and smiled. I nodded a hello and turned toward the students, noticing a hand up in the second row.

"Yes, Jasmine?" I asked as I wrote on the board.

"I already know I can't do this," she said loudly.

"Can't do what?" I turned around, annoyed that

the news of my impossible lesson had apparently spread through the building.

"I'm not allowed to do the national anthem," she stated, looking at her classmates for a reaction. Many of them ignored her and began whispering to one another.

I remembered this problem coming up once before in the two months I had been teaching. I remained calm and tried to be as politically correct as possible.

"Okay, I understand. Feel free to draw or read at the back table," I said with as much respect but as little drama as possible. Because I had a good friend who was Mennonite, I was extra sympathetic toward religious viewpoints that prevented students from participating. The time I had tried to do a spiritual, Jasmine had stormed out of the room and fumed in the hallway until I finally convinced her that I hadn't realized she was a Jehovah's Witness, and she was welcome to excuse herself anytime she felt uncomfortable. Though I'd made sure the issue did not come up in preceding lessons, I hadn't had time to digest this lesson or the obvious emotions associated with it before Jasmine entered the class. I looked at her and tried to show pleading vulnerability in my eyes. "Please," I thought, "just go sit down. No harm done."

Skeptically, she moved to the back table and began to sketch on some construction paper. I avoided her glance for the remainder of class.

OVER LUNCH, I considered what to do about Oscar. I thought about calling his mother or just sending home a copy of the music and a CD in hopes that would calm him down. I knew the issue needed to be addressed on a deeper level, though. It was hard to think of having a conversation with Oscar or his class about the issues surrounding immigration and citizenship when I was not even sure of my own viewpoints. All through college I had been the steady, sure liberal. How could I not have a defined belief on this?

Before my short lunch was over, Jasmine knocked on the classroom door, her face uncharacteristically kind. She handed me three books and a pamphlet.

"My mom just brought these up to the school," she said. "I called her at lunch." She pointed to the cell phone bulge in her pocket.

"Against the rules." I smiled and put the stack of materials on my desk. The last thing I needed right now was an attempted conversion.

"I know you already have the top stuff"—she took part of the stack and put it on my shelf—"but my mom forced me to give you some more. I want you to look at this, though."

I took the light brown book, and for a moment, my mind was distracted from the Oscar incident. One of the few hymnals I did not have in my personal collection was a Jehovah's Witness songbook.

"Can I borrow this?" I asked her without looking up.

"You can have it. My mom has a ton," she said, sitting at the other desk. "I was thinking, maybe I could choose an anthem out of there."

Of course, there was a catch. She wanted me to teach a Jehovah's Witness song in conjunction with the national anthem. I was lacking improvisational abilities today and wished both these situations would disappear. I began to respond with a certified, "No way," when I stopped. I remembered my friend and former roommate and her struggles with patriotism and religion.

"It must be hard," I began, "to have to sit in the back anytime I do something religious or patriotic."

She was caught off guard, as I'm sure she was ready to go on the defensive. "It's not that hard," she replied slowly.

"I am just thinking, you know, that you are making a choice to follow your religious views," I said, treading lightly.

She became defensive. "It's not a choice, it's my religion!" she exclaimed, back to her old stubborn self.

"I know, I know," I replied calmly. "I just wonder if it wouldn't be helpful if people understood this choice, or whatever it is."

"You mean tell people about my religion?" she questioned.

"I mean talk about your religion and other religions and other countries." I needed her support, not to complete the difficult task of a serious discussion, but to validate that I was doing the right thing as her teacher.

"And if we talk, like you say, about this stuff, then we could maybe learn some other songs, too?" And with that, Jasmine presented me with the opportunity to address her situation and Oscar's in the same lesson.

"We could maybe learn other songs," I replied, turning to my computer and wiggling the mouse. "Like other anthems."

She could tell I had lost track of our conversation and seemed pleased with what we'd accomplished. She got up to leave.

"Thanks, Jasmine," I called after her. She looked back and this time gave me a smile I could believe in.

AT THE END of the day, I assured Oscar that I would get him a copy of the lyrics and a CD to "The Star-Spangled Banner" over the weekend. "But we're not done talking about this," I said. He looked at me inquisitively and then became distracted by the last bell.

"Go ahead." I pointed at the door. "We'll talk Monday." When Oscar and the rest of the students had cleared out of the building, I hurried to my car, yearning for an opportunity to sit and think during the thirty-minute drive home. This weekend, I needed not only to find Oscar copies of our nation's song, but also to devise a legitimate strategy to defend my newest lesson. On Monday, I was going to enter into a conversation with the fourth through eighth grades suggesting that patriotism is a choice.

OSCAR'S CLASS DID not meet until Thursday, and by then I had ironed out the intricacies of my discussion. So far, no other teacher or administrator had confronted me about my controversial topic, and the students seemed responsive and not offended. Oscar's and Jasmine's classes would be the real test, though. I needed to make the national anthem both more and less than it really was: an old song written by a dead white guy that is the official song of the United States of America. When Oscar's class entered, I was ready. I rearranged the chairs in a circle and sat in a random seat with an American flag on my lap.

"Tell me, whether you were born here or not, whether you speak English or not, whether you stand and salute this or not ... " I held up the flag. "What does it mean to be an American?"

THE POWER OF ONE

Kathy Briccetti, PhD

"**H**OW ARE THINGS going on the playground?" I ask.

I'm meeting with our school's conflict managers—forty Asian, Latino, black, and white fifth graders—to practice the conflict resolution skills I taught them a couple of months before. The kids are spread out on the carpeted risers in the school's library, a mini-amphitheater, looking down on me as if I'm an actress onstage. For now they're quiet, but if I don't keep things moving, I'll lose them.

"Have there been many conflicts to resolve?"

A lanky girl with two braids raises her hand and then shouts out, "A first grader threw a dirt ball at me, so I threw it back!"

They've had some time to get over the excitement of carrying clipboards and wearing oversize navy T-shirts with a gold handshake logo, so today I'm hoping to work out any bugs in the schedule, see what they've forgotten, and role-play the conflict management steps again if they need it. Apparently, they do.

I love this part of my job as the school psychologist at this urban elementary school. Administrators have decided they'd like to see a reduction in tattling and suspensions as part of the district's antiviolence plan. I want even more.

When my own children attended a cooperative preschool where I worked one morning a week, they learned to "use their words." I know the power it can give kids when they solve their own problems. It teaches them much more than when adults do it for them or if they're simply punished over and over for playground squabbles. Our school's five hundred children are spilling out of the building into portable classrooms on the playground. We have bickering in lines, scuffles over kickballs, and occasional shoving matches to contend with.

My colleagues at the middle schools and high schools are dealing with students carrying weapons as well as breaking up fights, dispersing pumped-up crowds egging on the fighters, and calling police officers to come haul kids away. I want to reach elementary school kids now, teaching them how to handle conflicts without resorting to violence. I want them to see alternatives and learn new ways before it's too late and they are caught up in this thing that is so much bigger than they are; that is bigger than all of us.

"What do we do if the little kids run away from us?" asks a boy in baggy pants and an oversize basketball jersey. His name is Michael, and his mother is in jail for selling cocaine. His father has to work two jobs. Michael gets into several conflicts a week, no fistfights yet but he's come close. He is qualified for the gifted and talented program but his anger explodes out of him like a bomb, and I fear he'll get sucked into the cycle of violence we're trying to break. His teacher and I are giving Michael this privilege, the privilege of being a conflict manager, in the hope that he'll learn something he can put to use in his life.

"If they run," he asks me now, "do we chase 'em?"

With hands on hips and my head cocked to the side, I moan. I must have gone over this ten times during our training. Maybe it's too late for some of these kids.

But a boy in the back row answers correctly: "We ask a yard teacher for help."

So they did hear me.

Then a petite girl, sitting cross-legged in the front row, asks, "If the kids hit us, are we allowed to hit 'em back?"

This time I actually pull on my hair. "Hit them back?" I cry. "How many of you think you should hit them back?" Half the hands go up. A few shout the affirmative. The rest look confused.

"You're conflict managers! What do you think you should do?"

No one answers.

Another girl raises her hand. "My auntie told me if someone hits me, I better hit back."

I know the unwritten rules of their neighborhood. These kids don't live in the roughest part of town, but they still need to stand up for themselves. Unfortunately, that's often interpreted as fighting. I know parents who don't let their kids play in the front yard out of fear for their safety. Our school's neighborhood is still safe enough for bike and scooter riding, and kids play on the school grounds on weekends, but we all know about the drive-by shootings only blocks away. We have all heard about the drug dealers recruiting children. Here and now, kids do need to be tougher and, in some respects, grow up faster. Their parents are only trying to protect them, trying to inoculate them against some of the danger in the real world. This is not a new dilemma for me, so I tell the kids the same thing I've been telling kids for years:

"Not at school you don't." I shake my head. "What are conflict managers supposed to demonstrate to the other students?"

I'm met with blank stares, a few tentative hands.

"To talk about it," I say.

A couple of them shake their heads. "Then I'll be a punk."

"Besides"—I'm ignoring this last comment for now—"if you hit someone at school, you're no longer a conflict manager."

They know that two students have already been fired. When I heard that two boys I'd trained as conflict managers had gotten into an argument over who would carry the clipboard on their recess shift, shoving each other to the ground and fighting until two teachers pulled them apart, I was stunned. I was also embarrassed about my naïveté, wondering why I'd ever championed the conflict manager program in the first place. Where did I get off thinking a couple of days of training would trump the force of habit?

"And," I add to the group in front of me, "you'll get suspended." I'll convince them with this threat, I believe, but the girl in the front row speaks again:

"If I get suspended, my mama says, 'Oh well, you got suspended. At least you hit back.'" The kids murmur agreement and begin to talk among themselves.

I'm finally silent. I haven't heard this before. I had no idea that suspension was seen as a minor price to pay for saving face. I'm a middle-class white woman who was raised in a midwestern suburb. The closest I came to conflict was fighting with my brother over TV programs. But this is a no-win situation for these kids, one that clearly perpetuates the violence. I'm reeling a little but still believe that there must be a way to change it.

"Why do you think we have wars?" I shout to the group, aware that I might be getting a little carried away. "Why? Because everybody has to keep hitting back!"

I have their attention now.

"What's wrong with this? It won't ever end unless somebody ends it. Somebody's got to do something differently. We have to solve conflicts peacefully, with words." We've just celebrated Martin Luther King Jr.'s birthday, I remind them. They don't argue this point, and I take advantage, giving one last directive before letting them go: "Please just follow the script on your clipboard. Help everybody get along."

They leave, and I'm left to wonder, "Why am I doing this?" I am putting my time into teaching kids skills they aren't allowed to use outside of school and, worse, that put them in a bind if they do. It's times like this that I feel like quitting.

A week later, I see Michael on the playground during the lower-grade recess. I've heard his mother is out of jail and attending a rehab program, though his parents are splitting up and Michael has been in the principal's office twice this week. I know she's trying hard not to suspend him, but he's been refusing to work in class and has been calling his classmates names. Approaching me on the playground now, Michael is pressing the clipboard to his chest, his conflict manager shirt hanging almost to his knees. "Ms. Briccetti, I just resolved a conflict!" He's beaming. "These two boys were fighting over the tetherball, and I said, 'Do you want some help solving this problem?' And they said, 'Yes,' and I said, 'Okay. What seems to be the problem?'" His voice warbles with excitement, and as he drops his clipboard to his side, I can actually see him straighten up and stand a little taller.

"That's fantastic, Michael! And did they think up some solutions to their conflict?"

"Yeah, they're going to take turns. They decided that on their own." He's glancing around the playground, either looking for more business or trying to see who's noticing him. I can't tell which. "Now the little kids are following me around the yard, asking if they can help, too." His face is open, expectant.

"I'm proud of you," I say, hugging his shoulder to my side. "Maybe you'll be the one who starts to turn it all around."

He gives me a funny grin, as if he's humoring me, then struts off, clearly back on duty. "At least," I think to myself, "it's a start."

Unconditional Dedication

Erica C. Aguirre

I GREW UP IN Cerritos, a rather homogeneous area of Southern California. I am of Asian descent, as were many of my classmates, and as part of our Asian culture we were very diligent about our academics. Actually, we were downright competitive. When I made the decision to become a teacher, I wanted to complete my student teaching in the same community. If all went according to plan, I would spend my time helping students whose work ethic rivaled my own. I would be able to concentrate on curriculum and avoid the classroom management problems that sink so many new teachers. Everything went according to plan, but when I landed my first full-time teaching position, it was not in Cerritos. It was in a low-income, urban middle school with a large Hispanic and English language learner population.

My first year of teaching was one of many challenges not only with my students, but within myself. I was the dutiful student who was used to being very compliant with my academics, and I was used to working with students who were similar to me in that respect. My new students were pretty much the opposite. It was apparent right from the start that I was going to have a hard time connecting with these children. I just didn't know what their view on education was and if their families valued education. When people told me that school might not be a priority in the lives of these students and their parents, I turned a deaf ear.

"I will not lower my standards," I told Sandra, a colleague in my small learning community (SLC). Sandra was new to our school, having made the tremendous leap from kindergarten to seventh grade. With just one year's experience, I was the senior member of our SLC and charged with leading our group. Although it was exciting to take the lead, I was also very nervous because I knew how much I still had to learn. For example, experienced teachers seemed continually to get the most out of their students without lowering their expectations, and this was a skill I had not yet acquired. I was quickly coming to understand that expectations like mine had never been a part of my students' lives. I also had a feeling that no one had ever taught them how to achieve at a high level. During the first few months, Sandra and I spent far too much time together venting and lamenting:

"They *should* know to raise their hand to ask a question!"

"They *should* know that it's important to write their names on their papers!"

"They *should* know to take notes without being told, and to be able to write them in their own words!"

One day, though, I started to change my tune. I told, Sandra, "We can complain all we want, but until we teach them how to achieve, it just isn't going to happen."

"You're right." She smiled. "I'm seeing that that's true with seventh graders as well as with kindergartners." So I got to work.

I had in mind one student in particular. At the beginning of that year, I had gone against everything I'd been trained to do and think as a teacher: I'd decided that I had a least-favorite student. I didn't want to feel this way about Joey. "But he's really given me no choice," I told Sandra. He was a leader in the classroom, in all the worst ways. Being one of the more popular students, Joey could get the entire class to be so disruptive that it was nearly impossible for me to get through the day's lesson. Not only could Joey do this, but he could do it so covertly that it was hard for me to catch him and therefore discipline him. Despite Joey's behavioral issues, he had no problem with my classwork. I noticed that he was always one of the first students to finish the work, and Joey usually got every answer right. The situation with Joey bothered me even more knowing that he had so much potential as a student and that he was just throwing it all away to be the class clown. Needless to say, I wasn't spending much time on curriculum. I was spending all of my limited resources (mainly time and energy) on managing the class and, in particular, Joey.

I would also vent with Erin, another of Joey's teachers. I even got into the habit of referring to him by his last name, as if he were a soldier or an inmate.

Aragon this! And Aragon that!

One day, remembering my conversation with Sandra and the promise I'd made to teach all my kids how to achieve, I asked Erin if she thought we should call for a parent meeting.

"Definitely! I've just about had it with *Aragon!*" she said, mocking me in the special way that only a friend can.

I went to the dean of students, Mr. Anthony, and requested the meeting. He was supportive but said, "Joey Aragon?! Yeah, we can meet, but I don't know if it will help. We've had parent meetings before ... but it's a new year. We can try."

The day of the conference, Joey's mother arrived with a child whom she babysat to make some extra money. Mrs. Aragon spoke only Spanish, so the dean had to translate. We began the parent conference the same way we always begin them, by having everyone describe the good qualities they see in the student. Joey's teachers all said the same thing: "He has a lot of potential." Quickly, though, it turned into the worst conference I'd ever experienced, and it remains so to this day. Despite our positive comments, Joey slouched down in his desk with obvious attitude and disdain. Mrs. Aragon began to plead with Joey, and his response each time was to talk back to her, which in turn made her cry. There was no real result to the conference, no plan of action or new and improved system of accountability, but I wasn't ready to give up. Joey was about to encounter my stubborn side, the same personality trait that had helped me to excel when I was a teenager.

I held him after school and wasted no time asking, "What did you think of that meeting we had this morning?"

He sat silently, merely shrugging.

"Does it make you feel good, Joey?" I asked.

"What?" he inquired.

"To make your mother cry," I replied. "Does it make you feel like a big man? Because I can honestly say that a man doesn't talk back to his mother the way you did today. A man doesn't make his mother that upset in front of people she's just met. A man doesn't make the woman who gave birth to him, the woman who gave him life, cry."

Joey shrugged again.

I then told him, "You're lucky, Joey. Your mom will always care for you. Your mom will always love you unconditionally. You're lucky that no matter what, she will be there for you and will always do nice things for you. So I really hope that making her feel like crap made you feel good today."

He didn't straighten up in his seat or nod in agreement. He didn't even try to justify his actions. Obviously, I wasn't going to get much out of Joey, so I let him leave.

Not that I was going to give up on him. Quite the opposite, as a thought had occurred to me: If a mother can love her child unconditionally, a teacher can teach her students unconditionally. I wasn't a mother yet myself, but I was a teacher. I could do this.

Throughout the rest of the fall, Joey continued his bad behavior and his attitude got no better. Winter break, a much needed break from my students, came and went, and when I returned to school I expected to encounter Joey and his antics once again. But something had changed. Joey actually began to perform better in each of his classes. He behaved better, too, showing a polite side none of us had ever seen before. As his grades improved, so did his impact on my classroom. I began to praise him for all the little things he was doing well, in the hopes of encouraging even more good behavior. Soon he had the highest grades in my class.

"In my class, too," Erin told me. "Way to go, Aragon!"

Our school holds an open house every spring, and on the day of the open house, I approached Joey and asked if he and his mom were planning to attend.

"I'm not sure yet," he responded.

"I really think you should."

Joey asked, "What are you going to tell my mom?"

"I'm going to tell her you've been doing so well, Joey! I really hope you two come tonight because I think it would be really good for her to hear. For you, too."

I could hardly contain myself when Joey and Mrs. Aragon walked into my classroom. They approached me, and Mrs. Aragon immediately began speaking in Spanish. Finished, she looked at me expectantly as Joey translated her question.

"She wants to know how I'm doing," Joey said shyly.

With a huge smile on my face, I exclaimed, "Oh, my God! It's amazing! Joey is completely different now, and he's a wonderful student to have in class. He has the highest grade in my class!"

Joey translated, and the more he spoke, the more his mother smiled. She was tearing up, and when I looked at Joey, he had tears in his eyes, too.

That was pretty much a twelve-hour workday for me, but it was the best day of my career to date. Before the school year ended, I made it a point to ask Joey about his dramatic change.

"You were right," he said simply. "It just didn't feel good. Making my mom cry and stuff at that meeting we had wasn't cool."

I couldn't wait to tell Erin and Sandra, but nobody was happier than Mr. Anthony.

I have come to understand that my job is to take kids fresh out of sixth grade and prepare them for eighth grade. It is also my job to light that fire within, so that they strive not only to meet teacher expectations, but also to exceed them. I want my students to be proud, and as proud as I was of Joey, I will admit that I was proud of myself. I still have a lot to learn, but I'd taken a step in the right direction. Reflecting back on that second year of teaching, I knew that there would always be curriculum, but without giving Joey my unconditional attention and dedication, I would have failed in classroom management and I would have put a burden on my eighth-grade colleagues. This I could not do.

I have high standards for myself, just as when I was a student, and that is something I will never compromise. When it comes to meeting students halfway, though, I know now that I am capable of making that concession. It is well worth it.

◫

WHAT MY STUDENTS TAUGHT ME

Allison Anderson

I AM A LIFELONG learner. That's why I teach. If my students aren't teaching me something new, I might as well pack up the grade book and go sell encyclopedias.

I've learned my most important life lessons as a teacher. I've learned the value of education. I've learned what it means to be poor—and to make heartbreaking decisions. I've learned what it feels like to be judged by the color of my skin. And I've learned that all kinds of prejudices are real, and in order to teach students who are different from me, I need to listen and understand where those students are coming from.

My first teaching job was in Jersey City, New Jersey, right across the Hudson River from Manhattan. Jersey

City had suffered from "white flight" after the race riots of 1968. It was a blighted, poor city with pockets of gentrification, where I lived in a historic Victorian section—very white, very wealthy.

I worked as a contractor to the public school system, teaching emotionally and developmentally challenged students. Some were fresh out of "juvie" (juvenile hall). Quite an education for me. I had seven middle-school students, mostly black and Hispanic. These kids gave me a run for my money.

There was the leader of the pack, Orrin. Orrin hated me because I was a teacher and because I was white. Through the years, he had had one bad experience after another with teachers:

"Orrin, sit still."

"Orrin, why can't you behave?"

"Orrin, what's wrong with you?"

I called his mom to discuss his problems in my class, and she seemed to dislike me and mistrust me more than her son did. She didn't value teachers or schools, and Orrin had picked up on it.

Suddenly, I understood my parents' values and what they had always told me—education was the only thing no one could take from me. My dad had earned his college degree over ten years of night school, while he worked full-time to support his family of four daughters. Wow, I realized. My parents were right.

I treaded very carefully with Orrin because whatever he said, the rest of the kids did. I let him do his own thing, unless it was egregious, like complete disrespect. I had to be very patient, but he figured out my boundaries pretty quickly. He didn't want to completely piss me off, only toy with me. At thirteen, he knew how to work the system.

We didn't make eye contact for the first week. Then, gradually, he met my glance. One day, I picked up on one of his jokes—a gentle teasing of a Haitian student and how he had to swim to the United States because he was so poor (Pierre actually came over on a plane). When I made a gentle joke in the same vein about Pierre being able to outswim the sharks, Orrin laughed. No, he howled. And the rest of the class, Pierre included, followed.

From then on, Orrin was my bud. He teased me about being a teacher and being white, but in a respectful way. I teased him about being a pain in my neck, while making sure not to cross any lines. We had a lot of laughs, and he made sure the rest of his "posse" never disrespected me. In the beginning, I didn't get why he didn't respect me. I took it personally. But by trying to understand, and not getting caught up in judging why he did or didn't like me, I was able to find common ground for both of us. He taught me as much as I taught him. From Orrin, I learned that sometimes it's not about me.

I went from that job to St. Mary High School, also in Jersey City. I turned down an offer from St. Anthony High School, famous for their basketball coach, Bob Hurley, and the players he sent on to the NBA. I think St. Mary paid $17,000 as opposed to $16,000 at St. Anthony. This was 1993, when $15,000 was considered poverty level for a family of four.

At St. Mary, I got the education of a lifetime. After two months on the job, one of my best students, Jess, was out for two days. He came back and handed me a note from his mom. It was in beautiful script and a page long. To paraphrase, it read: "Please excuse Jess. His brother was killed in a drive-by shooting on Tuesday. He will make up all missed work. Sincerely, Mrs. M." (I still have this most disturbing letter.)

Jess was a first-generation American of Filipino parents. They were very poor, but education was so important to them that they managed to put together the tuition money Jess needed to benefit from the relative safety of a Catholic school. The older, less promising son went to Jersey City public schools, where he became involved with a gang. Jess fulfilled his promise and earned straight A's, then received several college scholarships. He was one of those quiet, nondemanding students, but I always gave him an extra push because it was clear, after the death of his brother, that he had the mettle to deal with whatever came at him.

I had one class I loved—they were so full of social, if not historical, insights. St. Mary was 40 percent black, 40 percent Hispanic, and 20 percent Asian, Irish, and other. (Then there were the two Mustafas, who were Muslims from the West Bank.) So we were very diverse. One day, the students decided to classify everyone by skin color. Not in a mean way, but in an ice-cream way. I was vanilla and so was Peter, who was from Poland. Yessenia was jamocha; Margarite and Pedro were coffee; Zainab was double chocolate. We all accepted our labels and laughed about them. We were all born different, and it was okay. Later in the year, I found a children's picture book about how people were different colors because we had been formed of clay and baked in the fire for different lengths of time. When I read it to the class, everyone loved that idea.

We were different in many obvious ways, but instead of politely ignoring those differences, we named them and enjoyed them. Those students taught me that given the right environment, even I, the white teacher, was allowed to appreciate differences out loud.

One of my most important lessons came from a class in which we were discussing the civil rights movement. I was explaining, in my scholarly way, how Martin Luther King Jr. fought for people to be judged not by the color of their skin, but by the content of their character. One black student challenged me: "Miss A, all white people judge other people by the color of their skin."

"Really?" I said.

"Really, Miss A. When you're walking down the street and a black man is walking towards you, you hug your purse and cross the street. Right?"

I was startled by the question, but in my heart, I knew the answer. "Yes and no," I said. "If the black man is wearing a school uniform or a suit and speaking normal English, I won't be so afraid. If he is wearing his pants at his knees, if he is being disrespectful, if he—or she, for that matter—is talking trash, I will be scared and avoid 'em. If the same guy is white, I'll be scared of him, too. It's all in the attitude."

My student had forced me to evaluate my decisions, to think about how and why I judge people. He taught me to stop and think about how many people unthinkingly judge strangers.

Another day, I sent a class to the school library for research. I arrived a few minutes behind them and noticed that the black students were sitting at one table, the Hispanics at another, and the Asians, Irish, and so on ...

"What are you doing?" I said. "You say you hate how people are prejudiced against you. But look at how you have segregated yourselves."

There was some general grumbling, but one voice rose above the rest. Arlena, whose parents were from the Dominican Republic, said, "Miss A, you gotta understand. We eat beans," gesturing at her table. "They eat fried chicken," pointing at the black table. "They eat rice and potatoes," pointing at the other table. "We all like each other, mostly. But we like what we know better," Arlena finished.

Someone called out irreverently, "Except for Peter. He's a Polack. He likes cabbage and beets." I was so proud that this black, inner-city student understood that cultural difference.

This young woman and her fellow students had taught me a universal truth—most of us feel comfortable with people who eat, speak, and live the way we do. The summer after this lesson, I took a trip that helped me understand.

I went to Russia to visit my college roommate, who was working at the *Moscow Times*. She knew some Russian, but she loved the end of the day when she came home to her American husband and they went to expatriate restaurants and bars and spoke English. My first night there, she took me to an expat restaurant. Even though everyone there shared the same experience of being in a foreign country, there was still segregation. The English speakers sat at one table, the French at another, the Germans at another.

After several days in Russia, I understood why birds of a feather flock together. It is exhausting trying to communicate in another language, another culture; my brain was constantly on high alert trying to figure out what train to take, how to order lunch, how to say "thank you" and "please." I was out of my comfort zone. I yearned for the familiar, the comfortable. I admit, I did go to McDonald's in Moscow. Those golden arches beckoned, and the cheeseburger tasted just like the ones in the United States. It was a taste of home, and it was very comforting. The only difference was that the Russians brought in their own vodka (seriously, there was a bottle on almost every table).

I am guilty of bias toward people who are like me. Bias is not wrong, it is a primal defense mechanism. But as an educator, I must recognize my own and my student's fears of things that are different. Different is okay, as long as we are not ruled by it. I thank a bunch of inner-city teenagers for teaching me that.

FIRST ROW, SECOND SEAT BACK

Cathryn Soenksen

MIGUEL WALKED INTO freshman English the first day of school, took the second seat back in the first row, and promptly put his head on the desk. He stayed in that position most of first semester. When he did agree to lift his head, everything about this burly defensive lineman dared me to try to teach him. His responses to any questions I asked were often in Spanish (might as well have been Greek to me) and would elicit guffaws from all the other Spanish-speaking students in the class.

Even given my specific assignment of teaching those students who were entering their high-school years reading and writing at a fourth-to-sixth-grade level, it was an exceptionally challenging year right from the start. The kind of frustration that accrues over years of falling further and further behind fellow classmates often manifests in behaviors that further complicate a student's chances of success. Several of my students entered ninth grade already in trouble with the law, four were regularly pulled out of my English class to meet with their probation officers, fully one-half of my kids were in special education classes because of learning disabilities of one kind or another, and 50 percent of my students were still learning English as their second or third language. Even in a team-teaching situation it was a challenging class, and many of my lessons had nothing to do with plot pyramids or direct objects.

And on the edges of it all sat Miguel, first row, second seat back, head down. Rumor had it that he hung on the fringes of local Hispanic gang activity, and his friends in class were those whom teachers had been warned to watch with a close eye. I assumed that the rumors were probably true and that his frequent sleepiness in class was the direct result of unruly late night activities. My notes to his mother apprising her of Miguel's lack of class participation never prompted a response.

Sometimes, though, Miguel would lift his head and fix his dark eyes on whatever activity we were doing, surprising us with evidence that he was actually tuned in to what was happening in class. That evidence, however, was often a grumpy commentary of, "This is so whack!" or a correct answer given in a sarcastic, belittling tone. I was constantly amazed that the limited work he completed (always just enough to skate by and remain eligible for football) was surprisingly good. Even his bare-bones writing had a distinctive voice and showed a deeper understanding of the content than much of the work turned in by our more "scholarly" students.

Occasionally, I caught a glimpse of the boy behind the wall of bravado he'd built around himself. One morning he arrived early, went to his seat, and took his usual position.

"Morning, Miguel."

A baritone grunt into the desk.

"Did you finish your reading last night or would you like to use this time to get your homework done?" I asked, confident that the answer would be no to both questions.

I heard a muffled, "Couldn't do it," from under his arm.

"Why not? Do you need help understanding the story?"

Miguel's head came up, and his eyes met mine, revved for battle. "Had to fix dinner for my sister and help her do *her* homework. Wanna know what happens in a chrysalis? I can tell ya. Wanna know what happened in that book of yours? Dunno."

I didn't do a very good job hiding my surprise. None of my assumptions about Miguel's life outside of school included cooking and caring for a younger sister. Ashamed, I realized that Miguel had ceased to be a kid in my eyes and had become simply an irritation, almost representative of every problem student I had. It was time for my problem students to become people again.

As my questioning evolved into actual conversation, I learned that Miguel had responsibility for his sister every night while their mother was at work. Every day after foot-ball practice, he rode the city bus home, fixed supper for himself and his sister, took care of helping her with home-work and getting her to bed, and then sat down to read the mail his mother, with her limited English, could not read. He was responsible for paying bills, returning phone calls, and answering any correspondence. He grinned as he explained, "You know all those notes you teachers send home telling my mom that I'm falling asleep in class and not doing my homework? She can't read 'em. They go straight to me ... and then straight into the garbage."

Thirty minutes earlier, I would have been enraged with the self-satisfied smile that lingered after he revealed that we teachers were just too stupid to have caught on to what he was doing with our communications to his mother. But now I was seeing a different Miguel behind the smirk. As he told me more about his home, his mother, and the sacrifices she had made to bring him and his sister to this country, I became the student and he the teacher. I gained both a new respect for his perspective on our English lessons and how he saw them as irrelevant to his life, and a new tolerance for his morning grumpiness and complacency. His words challenged my long-held, nar-row-minded philosophies and comfortable instructional practices. How could I teach these kids in such a way that they would begin to understand the power of education to transform their lives, their hopes, and their futures?

I had moved just a couple of years before from an ultra-rural, backwoods mountain community where the greatest diversity to be found was in the brand of jeans people chose to wear. The entire county boasted only one traffic light. My new position was in a city of multiple cultures and languages, where my blond-haired, blue-eyed, middle-class self found no frame of reference for relating to many of my multinational students. In Miguel's English class alone, students spoke five different languages and represented eight nations of birth. The diversity of a student body, I learned, brings both incredible richness and increased tension to class dynamics. I realized that if I was to teach my students effectively, I first had some learning to do about them.

At the beginning of the second semester, I shifted from teaching whole-class novels to encouraging students to select their own books to read. As I tried to help each kid find a book that would grab his or her interest and inspire passion, I learned that very few of my students had ever actually completed a book independently—or even been given the opportunity to do so. I also learned which girls preferred innocent adolescent romances and which ones related better to edgier characters. I learned which of my boys preferred fantasy and which wanted nothing but nonfiction. Some students chose books set in times and places completely removed from their own experience, while others had no use for characters that weren't mirror images of themselves. Miguel chose *The Maldonado Miracle* by Theodore Taylor and was quickly engrossed in a way I had not seen in him ever before.

"Why this book, Miguel?"

"The main character, Jose, is from Mexico, like my family."

Up to that time, Miguel had not finished reading anything assigned during the course of the year. To my surprise, my new problem became pulling his nose out of the book to participate in the rest of class, which, even more surprising, he did.

Before a week had passed, he walked into the classroom, most disturbed, to complain that the end of the book was "whack." He added, "That would never happen!"

"You *finished*, Miguel?"

"Yeah, but it shouldn't end the way he ended it. No way."

I hadn't read *The Maldonado Miracle* myself, so I asked, "How does it end?"

"It's stupid. Jose goes to all this trouble to cross the border illegally, risks his life trying to catch up to his dad, and then decides to go back."

"And you think that's stupid?" I asked, intrigued.

"Yeah. He comes here for a better life, to get an education, so he can be an artist, and then he gives it all up to go back to some fishing village. You don't just turn your back when you're handed a better life! Stupid."

When I told him I was looking forward to reading his summary when he turned it in, and encouraged him to include his evaluation of the ending, he asked if, instead, he could just rewrite the last chapter. Could this be the same Miguel who had protested even the simplest writing assignment for the entire first semester? This one who was voluntarily choosing to transform a simple summary assignment into an original narrative?

I did a little reading of my own that day, skimming through the book to see what had so grabbed Miguel's attention. The "miracle" referred to in the title occurs when Jose suffers a severe injury. While he is hiding in the choir loft of a small mission church, the blood from his injury runs between the floorboards of the loft, landing on the statue of Christ below. The entire town believes the statue itself has miraculously bled, until Jose confesses to the priest that the blood is his.

The next day, Miguel arrived with three pages of the new chapter and—gasp!—asked me to edit it with him so that he could write his final draft. Final draft? Miguel had not turned in more than one draft of anything all year. Within twenty-four hours, I had his polished fourteenth chapter of *The Maldonado Miracle,* along with a letter he planned to send to Mr. Taylor making recommendations for future books. In his rewritten ending to the book, Jose remains with his father in the United States, goes to school, and achieves his dream of becoming a professional artist, later returning to Mexico to paint that same fishing village as it was when he was a boy.

Miguel did not suddenly grow wings and a halo, but he did begin to take his own education more seriously, was scheduled into regular and college-bound classes, and graduated on time. He would pop into my classroom every now and again for a quick update, a high five before a big football game, or help with homework. I caught his eye at graduation and made sure he saw my enthusiastic applause as he stood on the stage with his diploma lifted high for all to see.

The following fall, Miguel dropped by school to tell me he was taking classes at the local community college. When I mentioned that I hoped my freshmen that year (another challenging crew) would find the self-motivation he had, he volunteered to come speak to them as one who had been in their shoes, headed in the wrong direction, but had wised up and found a better way.

The day of his volunteer talk he arrived with a button-down shirt tucked neatly into his khaki pants, new glasses giving him the appearance of a true collegian, and began, "Four years ago, I sat right there, first row, second seat back. I used to walk in and put my head down on that desk and stay that way for the whole class. Then I read this book..."

◫

TEENS ON THE
HIGH SEAS

Megan J. Koonze

A s I DIG through mounds of memories and cobwebs
in the basement in search of my old sleeping bag, I
begin to wonder why I volunteered for a three-day, two-
night "adventure" on the open seas—well, Long Island
Sound, anyway—with a group of twenty fourteen- and
fifteen-year-olds I have never met or barely know. We
have been in class for only two weeks, and this is a program to help transition freshmen to our school. I shake
off the pessimism and tell myself that all I'll have to do
is make sure nobody falls overboard as the tech teachers
and schooner crew members do all the work. In short,
my role as a diligent, albeit freezing cold, observer should
be fairly low-key.

The next morning, I give off one final yawn as I look over the diverse group of teens I'm about to embark on a journey with, most of them wiping the sleep from their eyes or checking for text messages one last time before we seize their cell phones. As I scan the sea of messy hair and overpacked bags, I notice Liz, a girl in my English class. I feel as though I barely know her. At this point, she is still just a first impression, the girl huddled in a seat set away from everyone else, her eyes focusing on her shoes, the fly buzzing around the room, the pictures on the wall ... anything other than me or her fellow classmates. She strikes me as the kind of student who would rather be anywhere but here, who lacks the drive and determination to be successful socially or academically in her new school. I realize I've never heard her laugh or seen a smile creep across her face; I wonder briefly if she even has teeth. As we begin to board the *Quinnipiac,* a one-hundred-foot schooner, I wonder how such a shy, unfocused student will make it through three days of manual labor and learning.

"If you see me put on a personal flotation device," Captain Jeremy tells the group, "it's a pretty good idea for *you* to put on a personal flotation device." Liz is tracing a pattern on the mast, and I repeat the message for her.

During lunch that first day, I watch as the students huddle together down low to stay warm from the salty, stinging breezes of the Sound. There are two main groups of kids, talking about pretty much the same things: how dirty they already are and how much it sucks to not have their cell phones. Liz sits away from both groups, her legs folded up inside her hoodie and her hat pulled low over her eyes. I have yet to see those teeth.

Just as she finishes her sandwich, I hear one of the ship's crewmen yell over the complaints of the students, "Okay, folks. Time to swab the decks!" The crew has kept the kids busy pretty much nonstop. A finger points to Liz as one of the four swabbers, and I watch her eyes widen beneath her hat. The look on her face is one of sheer terror, as if this crew member had just asked her to go down a roller coaster with no safety belt, which it would seem she'd rather do. He has to coax her up, but she does remove one leg, then the other, and finally her tiny hands from inside the comfort of her hoodie. As I watch her haul up giant buckets of water, I am amazed at the strength of her slender fourteen-year-old frame. I have to strain my ears to hear a barely audible, "Water coming down," as she gives the customary warning before sloshing her bucket of water across the aged planks of the *Quinnipiac*. Inevitably, some feet end up getting soaked as students and crew members shout, "Hey! Where's the heads-up?" They are smiling, though, and for the first time I hear Liz giggle. With each bucketful of water, her warning gets a little louder and a little more cheerful. It's wonderful to hear her voice stand out over the crowd, an achievement I'd become accustomed to by the end of our voyage.

We dock and then head to our campsite, where the afternoon team-building activities prove to be not only fun for the students, but highly entertaining for me as well. Watching boys try to throw one another over a raised rope

("Beware the electric fence!") and girls trying to leap eight feet to a "stepping-stone" made of cardboard and giggling as they roll through the dirt and grass was more fun than watching Larry, Moe, and Curly endlessly tormenting one another. Before I know it, we are a day and a half into the trip, my back is sore from sleeping on the rocky ground, my hair is greasy and frizzy, my face is permanently red from sunburn/windburn, and I am having the time of my life. I have begun to form relationships with fourteen students I'd never met before, and I am beginning to really get to know the six students in my class.

After watching my group slip, slide, and argue their way through half a dozen failed attempts at using their four "stepping-stones" to pass their group safely over the "river of lava," I was getting ready to save them from their metaphoric funerals on the banks of the river when suddenly I heard a newly found voice speak out over the mass confusion: "Well ... I have an idea." Nine scruffy heads swivel simultaneously, as if following one of Serena Williams' tremendous serves.

One of the loudest of the bunch raises his eyebrows and replies, "Whatcha got, Liz?"

Suddenly aware of all the eyes upon her, she squeaks out, "Uh, we could go down in groups of three, then have one student bring the stones back and go over with two more students and just like do that until everyone is over." I watch her eyes dart back and forth, from student to student, as if Serena and Venus are now volleying for match point.

A collective, "Oh, crap. How come I didn't think of that?" and then the congratulations.

"Sweet idea! Liz and Sam come with me first." The loudest boy picks up the lead again.

The smile that blossoms on Liz's face is, as Master-Card would say, priceless. She jumps forward with the two boys, and I watch the group float in perfect harmony through what had once been an overwhelming challenge, the river of lava. The fear I'd seen on Liz's face just moments before is replaced with dimples and giggles. I realize that this is the first time Liz has willingly made a suggestion, as opposed to me practically begging her to share one little idea from her daily warm-ups in class. It was worth the wait, seeing her gather the courage to address a group of loud, boisterous teens she'd never even met before the school year began.

After shivering through one final night in my tent, I wake up just before dawn and get the students out on the rocks by the shore to watch the sun creep up over the horizon. In pajamas and muddy sneakers, I hear the occasional "Wow!" and "Cool!" through chattering teeth. Several students say they have never seen the sun rise, blocked as it is by the crowded multifamily houses of New Haven. The night before, just gazing up at the stars was another first for many of the city slickers in the group. Some of the suburban students had helped point out constellations they recognized from stargazing in their own backyards. Now, they all had a shared perspective.

The first two days of "sailing" mostly involved the

engine pushing us through the too-choppy waters of the Sound, but we finally catch a break on that last morning—lots of sun and a slight breeze, perfect for sailing. The students are all excited as they realize they'll be able to raise the sails for the first time. The way they heave in perfect unison is almost surreal. Seeing these students learn and work so quickly and efficiently over the past few days has relieved my urge to jump in and help them with every little thing. With every new challenge they receive, I learn that they can do it on their own. Watching them complete the familiar tasks is further confirmation.

When I hear Captain Jeremy announce, "Ladies and gentlemen, we are about to enter New Haven Harbor," I am amazed at the big, "Awwwww!" that I, along with this now tight-knit group of teens, shout out. The one final task that needs to be completed is lowering and organizing the mainsail and foresail on top of the booms. Before I know it, five kids, including Liz, climb up onto the main boom as it sways slightly above my head. My heart stops temporarily as I imagine students bouncing off the deck like mosquitoes off a windshield, but I bite my tongue. I expect to see Liz equally terrified, but there she is, all the way out at the end of the mainsail boom, leaning against a rope as she tucks the massive sail into neat layers, working alongside her classmates. She squints to keep the wind out of her eyes, but her smile is as bright as the rising sun. I feel as if I am looking at a totally different person from the girl I met just two weeks before. My first impression has been happily discarded.

Captain Jeremy asks kids and adults to take a seat on the deck "and enjoy a few minutes of quiet. Listen to the sounds of the boat and of the water. Think about all that you have accomplished the past three days." Everyone does as they are told, and this time, I see Liz sitting back to back with another girl as they support each other.

While I was sad to see the trip come to an end, it was nice to go home and to get back to the classroom. "Hello, all. Did everyone enjoy a hot shower and a good night's sleep in your comfy beds?" I ask as they take their seats.

Liz says, "Yes," but she is smiling. I love seeing all those teeth!

Throughout that first period back, she quickly jumps into our discussions about the story we'd been working on. Several students compare anecdotes from the trip with some of the things the main character has survived. Liz is even willing to make a connection between her own life and the main character's. On top of that, she laughs at one of my corny jokes. Gone is the hermit crab who used to hide under her hoodie.

Over the weekend, I get an excited e-mail from Liz's mom. She gushes about the amazing transformation she has seen in her daughter, writing, "Liz came home from the trip and could not stop talking about the experience and about how much she loves her new school. She used to always be so quiet and wouldn't really talk about school. Her first two weeks, I couldn't get a thing out of her!" Liz's mom goes on to ask me if I have any pictures of her doing some of the amazing things she's been talking about, which of course I do. When I see her mother at "Meet the Teacher," I give her a dozen pictures of Liz swabbing the deck, hanging precariously off the boom, sitting with friends, and smiling. Her mom is so excited at Liz's new beginning that she gives me a giant hug, actually cracking my back as she squeezes. She tells me about all the different ADHD medications Liz has taken in the past, how she has always been so quiet and unfocused in school, and how she was nervous about going to a school where the students were all from different towns and the Havens.

"Now," she says, smiling, "Liz feels like she belongs at *this* school with *these* students. You don't know how much that means."

As I wish Liz's mother a good night, I begin to reflect not only on what Liz got out of the trip but on what I got out of it as well. I think back to when I was packing and how I saw my role as simple observer and sometime peacekeeper. I now realize that by being taken out of my element, the classroom, I got a whole lot more out of the experience than I expected. Just like what we'd hoped would happen for the kids. The chaperones wanted them to open up and experience things they never would have experienced otherwise, thereby helping them grow and think in new ways. Seeing students like Liz gradually reveal their true selves as they faced new challenges helped me see that sometimes you can learn more outside the classroom than inside it; that sometimes it's not about analyzing a specific poem or short story, but about analyzing who you are and how you can overcome obstacles, especially when being forced to work with others who may be from backgrounds vastly different from your own.

After the trip, it was easy to see that my personal bond with these students had grown tremendously. The teacher's work is never done, though, and the proof comes as the newly hatched social butterfly spends almost an entire class gossiping about the trip and her friends rather than focusing on the story we are reading. I meet with her and the assistant principal and outline the changes I love seeing in her, but I also point out the behaviors that are not appropriate for the classroom setting. All is resolved, and in her relationships with both me and her classmates Liz begins to think and act like part of an actual community of learners. Being in such a diverse school can be overwhelming for freshmen, and establishing a feeling of trust and togetherness is very important for academic success and the never-ending battle against truancy. Done right, this kind of team building can really have an effect on behavior and motivation within the classroom.

Now that a year has passed since our trip aboard the *Quinnipiac,* I can see that I was doing exactly what I always tell my students not to do: "judging a book by its cover." I had pegged Liz as the unmotivated, uncaring teenager who would never become passionate about my class. It took three bone-chilling days on Long Island Sound and two frigid, fairly sleepless nights at a campsite to realize that I needed to open up as much as she did. Liz, nineteen other students, and I all learned that struggling through new experiences together is, without a doubt, more powerful than reading about somebody going through new experiences of their own.

LA OPORTUNIDAD

Madeline Sanchez

S TUDENT TEACHERS OFTEN start out with a passion and a hunger to change the world yet are completely blindsided by the cultural shocks and academic politics that exist in most school districts. I believe many student teachers create this special, perfect little classroom world in their minds, and many of the teacher preparation programs that exist today don't prepare them for the real world of teaching. They may be taught all the academic techniques, like creating a lesson plan and following state standards in the curricula, but how can student teachers really prepare for the diversity that exists in schools today?

As an ex–English as a Second Language (ESL) student with non-English-speaking parents, I have always found it easy to be culturally sensitive and open to diversity. People develop an empathetic side and you learn, later on in life, that not everyone has developed this gift. Because it *is* a gift. Having a combination of this "cultural intelligence"—if such a term exists—and a proper education helped provide me with the tools I need to become a skillful teacher in today's society. It also allowed me to relate to my students, making their time with me and my time with them more meaningful. I do not believe that to be a good teacher you *have* to be of the same cultural or religious background as your students, but you do have to be empathetic and open-minded. Unfortunately, in some cases this may not be enough, depending on how diversity is embraced in the child's home.

I have heard a number of students say about me, "Oh please, she has no idea where we come from or what she's talking about." I have also witnessed parents of a kindergartner refusing to speak to a teacher or social worker about their child's issues because the teacher and social worker are "white" and can't relate to anything "about us or our child." I watched as this situation was defused by an African-American colleague who spoke on behalf of the "white" social worker, but what if this colleague hadn't been there? It's situations like these that teacher training programs don't prepare you for. Only instincts and life experience, plus a little luck, enable the young teacher to handle such interactions.

As a student teacher in an ESL level 1 (L1) high-school class, I was able to make a breakthrough this semester that will forever stay in my mind. Students of high-school age are a challenge to begin with, because it's at this age that many of them go through the "I know everything and I'm cool and you're not" mentality; however, I never imagined that L1 students would be a challenge. I know what it feels like to be a complete alien in an unknown place, where you have no idea what anyone is saying. It's scary and confusing. Today, ESL programs are much more efficient and much more tailored to the various needs of the individual students. Though I had ESL classes when I was young, it was really more of a sink-or-swim methodology. So to see ESL students today not working to take advantage of the multiple services offered to them is beyond anything I can grasp.

It is true, unfortunately, that depending on the child's environment, learning to speak English may no longer be a necessity. This was the case with my L1 tenth-grade student Tony. I started observing two things about Tony: First, he never wrote anything down; and second, he thought it was very cool to laugh and clown around with one of his classmates during lessons. Reprimands from the teacher didn't make him flinch, so I made it a point to interact more with Tony and actually started sitting between him and his friend so that they would literally have to talk around me. Tony spoke no English and could not read or write it, either. This made it even more mind-boggling that Tony wasn't interested in making an effort to learn English. My opportunity to really "get at him" came when I was asked to give him a test that required spelling, listening, reading, and writing. I knew taking him to the back of the room while a lesson was going on was not going to work, so I asked Tony to take a walk with me to the library. As we moved through the hallway, I started a casual conversation by asking how long he'd been in the States. Mind you, the entire conversation was in Spanish.

"How long have you been here?"

"*Dos,*" said Tony. Two.

"Two what?" I asked. "Two months, two years, two what?"

Tony answered, "Two years."

"Two years and still no *inglés?*"

Tony simply shrugged.

"*¿Por qué?*" I asked. "Why no *inglés?*"

"I don't want to," he said, shrugging again.

"Hmm. You 'don't want to.' Okay." I waited for a moment. "You have brothers or sisters?"

"*Sí.*"

"Which one? Brother or sister?"

Tony nodded. "*Un hermano.*" A brother.

"Oh, okay. Me too. I have a brother, too." I smiled, then turned serious again. "Do you speak English with him?"

"No."

"No? Why not?"

"He doesn't speak English."

"Why not?" I looked at Tony. "Does he go to school?"

"Yes. He just doesn't want to," he offered. Then, by way of explanation, "Like me."

"Oh, okay. How about Mom and Dad? They speak English?"

Tony walked a little faster now. "No."

"Mine neither." I hoped this would help to bridge the gap between me and my student. "But do they tell you to learn English?"

"Nah," he said with another shoulder shrug. "They don't say nothing. They don't care."

"Okay," I continued, "but do you care? About learning English? Do you want to or you just feel like you can't?"

Tony answered, still in Spanish, "I don't want to."

"You don't want to or you can't?" Tony was silent. "You know, I didn't know how to speak English either when I came here, but I had to learn because everyone around me spoke it." Tony was still quiet, but he looked surprised to hear this. "Do you want to go to college or find a good job that you like after high school?"

"*Sí.*"

"Well, you know, to do that you need to learn the language. Right now, it's easy because we live in Corona and everyone speaks Spanish here, but outside of Corona and where you live not everyone speaks Spanish. So if you know how to speak English, life will be easier for you. Knowing how to speak English and Spanish is a benefit for you, and it will help you find a great job that you like. So is it that you can't or that you don't want to?"

Tony admitted, "I can't."

"Yes, you can," I said, turning to look him in the eye. "And if you promise that you will come to class and try to pay attention, I promise you that I will help you. But you can't monkey around. You have to show me that you are trying, and I will help you even if we have to stay after class, okay?"

He caught me by surprise with how quickly he replied. "Okay."

"So yes, you do want to learn English?"

"*Sí.*"

I said in English, "All right!"

So we found a spot to conduct his test, and it was heartbreaking for me to see, as he completed it, that he was getting every answer wrong. For the read-aloud and spelling parts, I said to him, "What word does this sound like in Spanish?" hoping that cognates would assist him in getting a better score. Each time, though, Tony just wrote down an answer and then looked to me for approval or disapproval. But I gave him no indication either way, so he continued to fill in the blanks and eventually handed me his test. I knew he'd answered only one question correctly, so I immediately gave it back and asked him to try again. This time, we reread the questions together, and I pointed at key words in each sentence that I knew he had to know. With this tactic, Tony was able to read the sentences. I gave him praise in English and Spanish, using supportive phrases like "You see? You know!" and "*¡Muy bien!*" and even some tongue-in-cheek responses like "And you say you don't know English. Whatta liar!"

I have no problem being "uncool" if it means giving a student a smidgen of confidence. I could see little smiles escaping even as he tried to hide them. We were getting somewhere.

So Tony and I went through his quiz again, together. He still didn't pass the test, but his attitude afterward was completely different. I didn't have to ask him to sit away from that distracting peer; he would sit a desk away from him *and* leave an empty desk for me. Tony would also make sure to grab a dictionary as soon as he sat down. He paid attention and did his in-class work. Of course, every once in a while he would monkey around, but what high schooler doesn't? When he spoke to me in Spanish, usually to ask how to say a word or if his sentence was correct, my response was always the same, in English: "I don't understand you because I don't speak Spanish." This would crack him up and some of the other Spanish students, too. Tony would say in Spanish, "Ah, nah, miss. You lie!"

So what Tony would do was try different cognates for each word, saying them under his breath, and when he couldn't find the right word, he would use the dictionary. Or I would remind him to ask one of his peers.

At the time of this writing, I have until the end of the semester with Tony and his class—three more months. I already have a special place in my heart for Tony, and I really hope that our conversation was motivating for him. I truly hope he won't revert to his previous ways once I am gone.

My ability to relate to Tony on a personal level may be what helped me get through to him and may even help me with future students. I consider myself lucky for that. But the most important thing I know is to never make assumptions about students. We have no idea where their lack of motivation may stem from, and sometimes asking them in a humble, nonthreatening manner may be the only way to really get to the root of the problem. Like Tony, many immigrants today, young and old, don't see the need to learn how to speak English. Our culturally diverse city makes it easy to get through a lifetime speaking only your native tongue, and though this may be acceptable with older generations, it is a disservice to the younger generations. There is an English-speaking world outside our numerous little New York City communities, and being bilingual today is a benefit, so why parents would allow this is beyond my comprehension. The way I see it, all immigrants come here for the same thing: a better opportunity. And most want it for their children. So as long as I continue to encounter students like Tony, I will pose the same question to all: What opportunity are you really giving yourself if you come to the United States and don't take advantage of the free ESL education? What chance do you have if you never learn the language?

Steven and Me

Samuel R. Bennett, EdD

I AM A TEACHER. It is how I live, what I love, and who I am. Oddly, I am drawn to the student not expected to excel, the one labeled incorrigible or even an underdog. Hidden under rocky layers with unseen depths may be parents who are incarcerated, grandmothers as stand-in parents, or the grime of poverty. But always there is a glaring absence of positive role models. I want to offer these small, bitter nonconformists at least a short school year of encouragement. I want them to know they can improve both academically and socially. I want them to know it because I know it.

You'll recognize them. They are the children who carry a chip on each shoulder that is so heavy, I imagine it takes that raucous behavior to keep them afloat. I, too, have been guilty of reacting to the behavior instead of trying to understand its causes. And that is when I stop and remember Steven.

Steven entered my fifth-grade classroom for the very first time several years ago. He was recognized schoolwide as defiant and apathetic, and he set about reinforcing his reputation with zest. It was as though he were trying his very best to do his very worst. I reacted to the behavior, and our classroom confrontations were not pretty. A little research showed that Steven's previous teachers had fared no better. So I kept reading.

What I found was that Steven was being raised by a single-parent mom and had two older siblings. His dad had died when his mother was pregnant with Steven, just as they were preparing to leave Haiti. I wonder how often just knowing "the rest of the story" can change our perspective about a person—even one who seems like trouble. I considered whether Steven's apathy and poor classroom behavior might be a response to me being his first male teacher in elementary school.

My perspective totally changed with Steven once I started to view him as a young boy with loads of potential to succeed. Instead of my alien troublemaker, I let him become my "mission impossible," and I accepted the mission. I actively looked for ways to show interest in not only his school activities but also his extracurricular jaunts and even his family outside the classroom. My goal was to be less reactive to the behavior and more proactive to the person.

I truly believe in the saying "Our attitude determines

the attitude of others," so I began working from the inside out, trying to give Steven the boost that could jump-start his life. I visited his home and met his sweet mother. I found a strong and godly woman who wanted only the best for her children. Here was a mom who worked diligently as a Disney resort housekeeper in order to make great things possible in this new land she now called home. She traveled an hour to work each way, at least six days a week. Her schedule put Steven in never-ending after-school care. Steven's brother, Watson, was trying to make a go of community college, while his sister, Michena, attended high school and worked a part-time job. With a family busy trying to survive, Steven was on his own for success in school.

I tried working with Steven after school, and it wasn't easy at first. I asked him where he was headed in life, and his answer, "I just want out," broke my heart. Careful probing over weeks made a difference as I searched for ways to reach him. I will never forget the grin on his face when I told him I had been a police officer long before I became a teacher. "That's what I'm gonna be," he exclaimed excitedly. "I'm gonna be just like you, Mr. B." We had made a connection, however tenuous.

But Steven's behavior and classroom grades still needed work. He had never achieved any real accomplishments in school, and even his "perfect attendance" award was far more about his mother's perseverance in ordering him through the door than about any real effort on his part.

"I think you can make the A-B honor roll, Steven. How about giving it a try?" That was one of my earliest attempts, and I'm not sure I've ever seen such a pained expression of doubt on any child's face. His query, however, said it all:

"You do? Really?"

To have an adult believe in his ability to succeed was mind-boggling, yet Steven agreed that he would do everything possible to achieve that honor. I'd like to say he made it and lived happily ever after, but the truth is that he worked harder than ever the next few reporting periods—and remained unable to accomplish the honor roll feat. The further we got into the year, the more his small body seemed to sag with unrewarded effort.

During the last nine weeks, I worked harder, too. As he would leave my classroom at the end of the day, I would say, "Steven, make sure you complete all of your assignments and study for tomorrow's spelling test."

He would stand taller before my eyes and reply, "Yes, sir."

And each morning, I would call him to my desk and show him how his grades were improving. My goal was to provide Steven with a constant reminder that he could accomplish his dream. I encouraged him; I cheered him; I loved him.

Steven's behavior showed constant improvement as I began to plan a fifth-grade graduation field trip to Cypress Gardens amusement park. I had informed my class that attendance would be determined by positive classroom behavior, and I used a color card behavioral management plan to define success. The number of card pulls could lead to a time-out, a note sent home, a call to parents, or, when all else failed, a visit to the assistant principal's office. I told my students that anyone with a referral to the office during the last nine weeks would not be invited to attend our Cypress Gardens trip. Oops!

Everything looked good until a few weeks before the trip. That's when Steven got into a fistfight with another student. Fighting was an automatic referral, and I almost cried as I wrote out Steven's office referral. I thought to myself, "He has made such improvement, and I am so disappointed that this has happened." I even thought about not sending Steven to the office and handling this in the classroom, but sometimes "tough love" is the only and best approach. Steven left my room with his head low. He was moving very slowly toward the office; clearly, he knew how disappointed I was in him that day. Worse, our school's zero tolerance for fighting meant that Steven and the other student were both suspended from school because of the fight. Steven served his time and returned to school without incident. His behavior was now impeccable.

With the final plans for the Cypress trip under way, I was still trying to rationalize Steven's fight. I wanted an excuse to allow him to attend our trip. I even talked with my other grade-level teachers, who thought I should make an exception to the rule. After all, we reasoned, for Steven this was a once-in-a-lifetime fifth-grade graduation trip.

The other kids wanted him along, too, having watched his progress with pride. But I knew how often I had told my class, "Say what you mean, and mean what you say." I choked back my own tears as I told Steven that he would not be able to attend our trip because of the office referral. Gosh, I wanted to let that kid go. I made arrangements for Steven to stay with another teacher on our trip day, and off we went. It was a great day, although bittersweet for me.

We marked the year's end with the usual awards ceremony, but this one was different. Steven had won. I felt as proud as a dad when I called his name. At long last, he had made the A-B honor roll he had worked so hard to achieve. It was a first for Steven and an accomplishment he would remember forever. I watched his shining face as he strode toward the front, and I think my chest swelled bigger than his at the cheers from his peers. They, too, had witnessed a miracle. Steven's second award, as Turnaround Student of the Year, came from the teachers as a whole. This wise and wonderful group had not judged his future on that one fight, but instead had rewarded his entire year of progress.

Of course, this was also the day I was sending off my fifth graders for their last summer before entering the world of middle school. Thus, I planned a final day of learning and celebration. Many of them I might never see after this day, so I wanted to give each of them a personal letter that would include the poem "People Who Achieve Their Dreams Have These Qualities in Common" by

Susan Polis Schutz. I was called to the principal's office before I could read them my from-the-heart message, and I went, fuming at the interruption.

To my shock, I walked into flashbulbs and hurrahs—and the news that I was a top five finalist for Florida Department of Education/Macy's Teacher of the Year. This was one of the finest moments of my life—beaten out only by the births of my own children and my wedding day. But what I really wanted was to read my letter to my "kids."

The reporters and others followed me back to the classroom. They watched as I started to read, but my voice choked and my eyes filled. This was my last day with these students, and I wanted so badly to have made a difference. My wife, Debbie, read my letter as I listened and reflected on this fifth-grade year.

But reporters have to make a living, too, and they swarmed to interview my fellow teachers, administrators, staff, and students. And in doing so, they changed my life. Because the reporter who spoke with Steven asked him, among other things, why I was a good teacher. Steven said, "Mr. Bennett expects all of us to do our very best. He encourages us in everything we try and do." Then, out of the blue, Steven blurted, "I wish he was my dad." Those six words sank deep into my heart that day, and they still live there today.

I call Steven my unofficial adoptive son. He has become part of my life, and I have become part of his. In my twenty-plus years of teaching, I have had many honors bestowed upon me, but those six words remain my greatest award. They are one small boy's belief in his own ability, but they represent a generation of children who need the chance for success that only we teachers and believers can offer.

We must view students as what they can be and can become, regardless of how deeply that is buried. Many people did not expect Steven to be successful. At first glance, he was simply another little Haitian boy who would depend on the system. I saw him as a success in the making—because I am a teacher. Today, I see Steven able to achieve success in whatever he desires as long as he, like all of us, stays focused on his goals.

That summer, my son, Jeremy, and I planned a special trip for Steven. We wanted to reward him for being the Turnaround Student of the Year. And what else? We decided to take him and a friend to an all-day trip to Cypress Gardens amusement park. I reminded Steven that this was not a replacement for the graduation trip he'd missed because of the fight, but a reward for his year-long improvement in both academics and behavior.

Steven left my class after fifth grade, but he didn't leave my heart. I will remember those six words, "I wish he was my dad," forever. I will teach harder, listen more closely, and perhaps care deeper, because I know now that I can make a difference because I am a teacher.

When I visited Steven at his home after his first day in middle school, "just to see how it went," he showed me his many books and the first-day survey from one of his classes. One of the questions was, "What is the happiest day of your life?" Steven had written, "When my fifth-grade teacher told me I made the A-B honor roll." Wow! Of all the days of his life, this was his happiest. Steven gave me that paper, and I cherish it in my Steven file.

As Steven continues to grow and achieve, I am staying involved. I began working on respect with Steven in fifth grade, and I have continued into high school. And he gets it. He said recently, "Mr. B, people want to be with us and around us because we treat them with respect, you know?" And I agree, unequivocally.

For us teachers, it is the respect we show students that makes them want to be in our classes. When you respect others, it has the old "ripple effect." It just keeps happening: Give respect, receive respect. It is reciprocal. I want Steven to respect his family, friends, and those in authority, because that will lead to his success.

Today, Steven is running track and playing football, so I invested in his life with some weights and dumbbells. He is beefing up and becoming very athletic in his sporting events. I recently attended one of his high-school track meets where he didn't win, but he did finish the race. My advice to Steven was simple: "Don't quit; keep training, and victory will come." Like his goal of making the honor roll, it may not happen overnight, but tenacity will win out.

I want to be Steven's best cheerleader and encourage him to succeed. There will be times when he may just want to quit. My job is to help him develop that stick-to-itiveness that lies within all of us—because I am a teacher. It is what I do, and I love every minute of it.

In April 2006, I was walking across the White House lawn, preparing to enter the Oval Office to receive greetings from President Bush, who was honoring me as the 2006 Florida Teacher of the Year and one of four National Teacher of the Year finalists. My wife, Debbie, turned to me and said, "Sam, aren't you glad you didn't quit? You didn't quit the bachelor's degree, the master's degree, the doctorate, and you didn't quit teaching—and look at God's unfolding of your life as an educator."

She's right. I am glad that I have the tenacity it takes to stay the course and never quit. I pray you will, too, and that you will enjoy every minute of the teaching you do. I give God all the praise and glory for the encouragement that I have received along the way. For Steven and for every child whose life we touch, I want that same tenacity. Let's teach them to dream big dreams and help them see those dreams come true.

◫

BEYOND BOXES:
HOW TODAY'S STUDENTS
DISABLE LABELS

Kerstin Rowe, MEd

THERE IS NOTHING worse, as a white teacher, than to be called racist. So when a highly paid consulting group brought in to help our district close the achievement gap told me what I had to do, I did it.

My students proved them wrong.

THE HIGH SCHOOL where I taught basic through advanced placement (AP)-level English stuck out like a sore thumb in our district. The other five high schools were largely Caucasian (approximately 85 percent), drawing from high socioeconomic neighborhoods. My school, Washington High School, was the black sheep. Our student body was

27 percent Hispanic, 38 percent black, 29 percent white, 5 percent Asian/Pacific Islander, and 1 percent Other. The school also had a strong Muslim population. We had students who had escaped from Sudan and Somalia; students whose parents were immigrants from Armenia, Ethiopia, Palestine, you name it. Many of my students or their older siblings were born in other countries. Having grown up an hour from New York City, I relished this diversity. I had taught in 90-plus-percent Caucasian schools, and I disliked the literal lack of color in my classes. At Washington, I loved learning about different kids, their backgrounds, and how to properly pronounce their names.

So when the district brought in experts to teach me how to better reach and teach my students of color, I jumped at the chance to be trained in what they called "culturally responsive instruction." I was the first teacher from my school to volunteer for, and be placed on, the TLC Team—a group of administrators and teachers who would meet all day for six days during the school year to become trained in methods devised to close the achievement gap. I was excited about this training. I was already a good teacher, and I wanted to be better. I wanted to be an integral part of changing the system for the betterment of all students.

The experts, Pioneer Achievement Consultants (PAC), told us that with the right training we would become culturally competent teachers. We would learn not to unintentionally alienate our students of color because we would plan, and thus instruct, accordingly. We would gain a deeper understanding of the different perspectives and methods of learning that our students of color brought with them to the classroom. We were told that we needed to see race first, beyond everything else about the student. We were told that if we didn't see race first, we were fooling ourselves and practicing racism in a deeply destructive, underground manner.

In our new postmillennial society, I, a white female, was ready to believe and learn from the black and Hispanic PAC trainers. I had worked with many students of color up until this point in my career, with quite a lot of success. I had lived a year in Benin, West Africa, experiencing the life of a minority there as a white female. I had thought and studied a great deal about race and race relations before I joined the TLC Team, but I knew I was no expert. I wanted, and thus sought out, more knowledge. I wanted to learn how to defeat racism in the classroom.

AFTER SEVERAL DAYS of training, PAC asked us to go into our classrooms and implement their suggestions, one of which was finding out how the students identified themselves racially. They said that we needed to do this directly, up front. They said to ask the kids. They told us that all people of color possess a strong, clear racial identity, beginning around the time of middle school, and that we teachers needed to know how our students identified themselves in order to understand and teach them effectively. I was told that knowing the answer to this question would increase my cultural awareness of my students; that knowing the answer would increase my rapport with my students; that knowing the answer would make me a better teacher.

But I was skeptical. I felt that I already had my gold mine: in the wonderful uniqueness of each of my students and in the relationship I had with them. By this point in the year, the students and I knew one another well. We trusted one another. They knew I was a tough teacher, but that I was also someone who treated them with respect and understanding. They knew I was on the TLC Team, learning about techniques to close the achievement gap. Given Washington's population, it was impossible to escape the issue of race. It was everywhere. And while I didn't know how all my students identified themselves racially, I knew their backgrounds, where they were from, and, for most of them, where their parents were from. I knew which teams they were on, and I'd ask how their games went the day before; I knew who was in the school play or in orchestra, and I'd ask about rehearsals; I knew who worked at Papa Murphy's Pizza, and I'd ask how closing went the night before. That is why I was skeptical of how much knowing their self-appointed racial identity would help me, but I was ready to push aside my cynicism and jump right in, wanting to trust what I had been told. Plus, I was interested, as always, to hear what my students would say.

I WALKED INTO class that day determined to carry out my mission. Considering my student population, I figured it would be easy: an AP language and composition class of twenty-six motivated, intelligent, ethnically diverse juniors. Of all the kids at Washington, the students in this class would really be ones who could answer the question I had been told to ask. Of course, we would be able to discuss the issue in all its complexity.

I told my students straight out that the TLC Team had an assignment for me and that I needed answers from them.

I asked: "How do you racially identify? Not how do others see you, but how do you see yourself, racially?"

I held my breath.

Silence.

Instead of releasing a flood of racial histories, my students were quiet. Then some kids asked, "What do you mean?"

Right off, I realized my students were not as racially aware as PAC had led me to believe. I told them, "The question is not what country are you from, which would be your nationality; or with which ethnic group you identify, which would be your cultural group, like Irish; but your racial identity—like Caucasian, African-American, or Hispanic." I paused. "The way you see yourself," I added, using PAC's idea that all persons of color identify themselves by race first and foremost, beyond anything else.

My few white kids quickly answered, "Caucasian," and seemed to be done with it. But they listened intently for their classmates' responses, knowing this was a charged issue. My students of color remained silent.

So I asked Ayana, one of the smartest students I've ever taught and one of the most honest. She was born in Ethiopia, but her family were refugees in Kenya for the better part of her childhood before moving to the United States.

Ayana answered, "African."

I said, "Well, that's the continent you're from. Do you consider yourself African-American?"

"No," she said. "I'm African. Okay, Ethiopian. But now I'm American."

"Those are still nationalities. Would you say you identify as black?"

"That may be what people refer to as the color of my skin, but I don't. I think my skin is brown. I'm African."

Okay. I decided to move on and keep this line of thought open. Next I asked Pablo. Pablo had one Caucasian parent and one parent of mixed descent (African-American and Mexican).

"Pablo, how do you racially identify?"

"Uh ... I don't. I'm just me."

"Hmm. PAC, this group I'm working with?"

"Yeah ... "

"They said every teenager totally knew how they racially identified. What do you think of that?"

"Well, it's just never come up. I'm just Pablo. I identify as Pablo."

"So, you don't identify as Caucasian?"

"Nope."

"African-American?"

"Nope."

"Hispanic? Latino?"

"Nope. Just mixed, I guess." He chuckled.

"And it's never come up?"

"Nope. I'm just me."

"Okay. Fair enough…"

My class jokester, Ted, who sat in the next aisle, piped up, "He's Afri-Mexi-white!"

Kids laughed.

Next, I asked Maria, whose father's parents were from Spain and whose mother was from Puerto Rico. Maria was a beautiful, strong young woman. Most of my (white) friends meeting her would probably identify her as Hispanic. So I asked, "What about you, Maria? How do you racially identify?"

"I'm part Puerto Rican and part American. My grand-parents are from Spain."

"Would you use the terms Hispanic or Latina to iden-tify yourself?"

"No! Latina means from Latin America, which I'm *not!*"

"What about Hispanic?"

"No. I'm not from Mexico. I am part Spanish and part Puerto Rican."

I could sense Maria's resistance and frustration with the issue. Why was I trying to cram her into a box? Con-trary to what I'd been told, pushing Maria to racially identify herself was harming our rapport.

It was also clear that neither she nor Pablo had given their racial identity a great deal of thought besides being proud of their heritage. They were much more concerned about their individual identity.

Hmm ... I felt stuck. Typical me, I decided to delve deeper, not easier. I turned to a student of mine from Armenia. He was a very laid-back, very intelligent young man. When I asked his racial identity, he just shrugged.

"I don't know. Caucasian? No, I guess not. I'm American. But I'm from Armenia."

The class looked at me. They looked at him. None of us had answers.

"Okay ... so no one is fitting too clearly into these labels. That's fine.... Let's open it up. How do you identify each other? What about David? How does he racially identify?" I asked the class. David, a bubbly, popular student, looked very typically Greek: dark curly hair, dark eyes, olive skin.

"Caucasian!" called out one student.

David: "Dude. Do you *see* my skin? Does it look white to you?!"

"Greco-Roman!"

"I'm not Roman! I'm Greek. That's what I am. Greek-American."

"I'm Mayflowerian!" This from Ted.

"Mrs. Rowe?"

"Yeah?"

I turned to look at Alyse, a petite brunette student from Georgia. As in Georgia, Russia.

"Am I Russian or Georgian or Caucasian?"

"I'm Georgian, from right outside Atlanta!" piped up one of my two blond girls.

"Mrs. Rowe?"

"Yes, Ayana ... what do you think?" I knew Ayana would have something insightful to say, something that might bring some closure.

"This is pointless." Heads nodded in agreement. She continued, "Why do we have to fit into these boxes? It's bad enough when we have to fill in those little bubbles on standardized tests asking us our background."

Maria said, "I just always bubble in 'Other.'"

"Yeah, me too," said Pablo.

Maria continued, "It's 2005! The world is increasingly global, with all sorts of people meeting each other and marrying and having children. Boxes are so last century."

From around the classroom, there was a chorus of, "Yeah!"

I turned back to Ayana. She had more to add.

"It's dumb. So many of us are from mixed parentage or from other places. There are too many different kinds of people to have so few labels. And didn't we learn in, like, kindergarten that calling people by labels is bad?"

The class concurred. We all felt the exercise was fruitless. It was much more important to treat one another as we had been for the whole year so far: as unique beings from a variety of backgrounds. Backgrounds that sometimes, but not always, had bearing on our current lives. It was obvious that mostly this was a group of teenagers who looked different from one another but were all intelligent, caring young adults. And they all wanted to be treated as unique individuals, regardless of their ethnicity or the color of their skin.

The "expert" from PAC didn't like it very much when I brought back my findings to the group at the next TLC Team meeting. My report didn't fit neatly into his pre-scribed lesson plan. Much of the training was interesting for me from an intellectual and theoretical point of view. But when it came to implementing their suggestions, I kept thinking of my kids, and I balked. I knew PAC's advice wouldn't fly with them.

I felt PAC offered only black-and-white solutions, asking us to PAC kids into certain holes (puns intended). My students, ever part of our changing, modern, multiracial society, do not fit into defined holes. Nor do they wish to. Maybe not every student resists racial identification and labels, but mine did. As a matter of fact, most students I've taught resist labeling. I think they can teach us a valuable lesson. People defy boxes. Each of us is a unique being. And we'd each like to be treated as such. That's a lesson even those highly paid consultants need to learn, and quickly, if they are going to help anyone close the achievement gap.

To this day, I often think of Pablo, who proclaimed aloud in class, "Why do I have to be one of those boxes? Why can't I just be me?"

Indeed. Why not?

THE INVISIBLE KNAPSACK

Rebecca Branstetter, PhD

S CHOOL PSYCHOLOGISTS CARRY many things—literally and figuratively. We carry the responsibility of making sure that we understand what makes a difference for students. We must know what interventions are appropriate for each individual child, be able to uncover undiagnosed disabilities, and use care not to misdiagnose students. We also carry a zillion bags of test materials to make sure we get it right.

I didn't realize I would also carry with me all of my unchecked biases toward working with diverse student populations, until I was in my first year as a school psychologist in San Francisco. I know, you think of San Francisco as this beautiful, iconic, rich city of fun (wheeeee!

cable cars!), but there is another side to San Francisco. I had never seen this side until I was assigned to the Bayview district.[1] I was right out of graduate school and ready to make a difference with my brand-new credential. I was not swayed at all by the fact that I would say the name of the school I was assigned to and colleagues would instantly look as if they were smelling something bad.

My prior experience with "urban America" and "diversity" was shaped by movies in the 1980s in which tough street kids found their way into fame and acceptance through the power of dance. Dance transcends race! Or I had experienced movies in which a nice white lady goes to the school and with radical teaching methods (such as "listening") transforms the lives of poor children of color. While I didn't really expect to see the Crips and Bloods engaging in *West Side Story*–esque dance-offs while the nice white lady showed them the way with a pencil and a pep talk, I really didn't know what to expect.

My first day, I sauntered up to the middle school campus and found the front door bolted with forty-seven million chains and padlocks and no one in sight to open it. While the sign out front read, "Welcome Back to School!" the door said, "Get the Hell Away from Our Fortress!" I managed to peer through a barred window to gain the attention of a secretary and was let in for the first training of the day.

---

[1] Bayview! Sounds so pretty! Not pretty. Pretty dismal, actually. I was shocked that I was still in San Francisco.

I was wearing my most respectable outfit—crisp gray pants, black turtleneck, and the cutest little red kitten heels with accented red headband. I know! Cute, right? I thought the outfit said, "I am professional and stylish. While I am only twenty-four years old, I am clearly competent and knowledgeable beyond my years." Turns out my red kitten heels and headband actually said, "I claim the Norteño gang!" But I looked so cute.

The first day of school, I was directed to my janitor's closet—I'm sorry, *office*—and I set down all my bags of test kits, files, and neatly organized binders of resources. As a school psychologist, I knew how to link students to resources. I had even filed the resources by zip code, so I could locate the resource closest to the family residence. Take that! I had a cross-filing system by themes as well.[2] One particular tab that I had carefully color-coordinated and filed was from a guest speaker in a class I had just taken in my final year of graduate school. The topic was diversity. It was a one-day thing, in which the presenter had us do a variety of cultural sensitivity activities.

All of my classmates were (and I guess still are) white.[3] At this event, we were asked to write down when it was that we realized we were "white." Um … I guess right now? I grew up in suburban Colorado. Everyone was

---

[2] Of course I did. Nerd alert!

[3] True story: My dissertation committee had a long-running argument about what to call the white kids in my research sample. Caucasian? Caucasian-American? European-American? They did not seem amused when I suggested "pigment-challenged." Humph!

white except Laurie and Geoff, the two black kids at my school. The term *African-American* was just coming into vogue when I was in high school, and people whispered it as if it were cancer. As in, "That's Laurie, she's African-American." My people were not comfortable talking about race for fear of being politically incorrect or insensitive. This was a pre-Obama world, in which we declared everyone "Americans" and pretended race was irrelevant.[4]

The point of that activity was that we pigment-challenged individuals typically do not have to confront our own racial identity because we are part of the dominant culture. Let's face it, no one fears me when I get on public transit late at night, old ladies do not clutch their purses a little tighter when I walk near them, and I can get a cab in 2.2 seconds. Every time the news reports on a crime, I don't have to hear, "The suspect was a five-foot-five-inch white woman in her twenties." There is no cumulative effect of having to see white women continually being cast as a nefarious character in every movie or TV show. We carry around with us, as the instructor put it, "an invisible knapsack of white privilege," in that we do not have people judging us by our race. If there are judgments, they are more often in the positive direction. Seems I had one more thing to carry with me—a new awareness and an invisible knapsack.

---

[4] One could argue that much of America still tries to be "color-blind," even after we voted in our first African-American president. Discuss among yourselves.

In retrospect, one would think that at UC Berkeley we would have had more than one day of diversity training. Perhaps we were meant to obtain cultural awareness by osmosis, since Berkeley is most certainly a melting pot of every type of person on the planet. To my graduate school's credit, I *had* read a million articles about the importance of considering racial and linguistic diversity in everything we do. I had read all about the overwhelming overclassification of African-American boys in special education. I just didn't really have a context for how to apply my newfound "awareness" in my everyday job, when nine out of ten referrals for special education were African-American students. I wasn't yet equipped to conquer my school, let alone the nation's racial ills.

Like any good student, I had researched the demographics of students in Bayview before arriving: 70 percent African-American, 20 percent Latino, 10 percent Other. Ninety percent of the students were below poverty level. I added the data to my resource binder, and I was excited to get crackin' on saving the children. I was feeling more and more like a younger and cuter Michelle Pfeiffer already. There was this one invisible knapsack situation weighing me down a bit, but any school psychologist with multiple school sites knows that we just have to carry a lot of crap in our jobs.

That first day when students arrived, I couldn't wait to make a difference. I was armed with research! and pluck! and a newfound cultural awareness! The first student I saw was an eighth grader whom I will call "Darren." You could not miss Darren. He was already clearing six feet and probably in the 152nd percentile for weight, if that's even possible. If you saw Darren on the street, you might think he played professional football. He was like a thirteen-year-old linebacker, and this particular linebacker had a learning disability, as I later found out when trying to locate kids on my caseload.

The first time I pulled Darren out of class, it did not go well. I came into his classroom and asked if I could see Darren for a moment. He screamed, "I didn't do it! Get away from me, you white bitch!" I'm not sure what he was talking about (and how did he know I was a bitch?), but I assured him he wasn't in trouble. He grudgingly came with me and did not say a word as we walked to my janitor's closet. I tried to engage him in small talk. Nothing. I tried to explain, in a very kid-friendly manner, what we were going to do together. Nothing. No response. I told him that we could work together on another day if he wanted to pick a good time, and he snorted, "Fine. Whatever," and skulked back to class.

I tried for three straight weeks to get Darren to work with me. Every time I came to the classroom, he screamed at me. One time it was, "Go away! I ain't no fucking special ed, bitch!" Well then. I did not have anything in my resource binder under the tab "This kid hates me and I don't know why." I was relentless, though. I wasn't giving up. I looked through his records to get more insight. Everything was going pretty well for him throughout elementary school. Then, when he got to middle school, written all over every piece of paper were the telltale words of a kid who did not have many positive interactions and had gone quite some time without receiving any positive reinforcement. He was described as "disrespectful," "defiant," "unmotivated," and "hostile." What had happened in just three short years?

A few weeks later, as I drove up to my decrepit, deadbolted school, I saw Darren walking in the same direction. He was quickly shoving something in his backpack, and his eyes were darting back and forth as if he were hiding something. He had just passed a small corner store, and for an instant, I thought, "Oh great. He probably stole something." Then I remembered my graduate school class, and I was ashamed for making such an assumption. Yet I was curious. What was he up to?

I parked my car, and as I got out all my materials from the trunk—wait, did I remember my invisible knapsack of white privilege?—I saw Darren scurry by me through the back door. Suddenly, I was a far cuter version of Columbo, on the case. I followed him in, and we met up in the stairwell. Towering over me, he said guiltily, "Erm. Hi, Ms. B." And then his backpack meowed.

Darren had smuggled in a kitten. His nefarious plan was to save this kitten that he had found on the way to school. Darren said in a soft voice, "I just found her, and she was all alone, and she looked hungry. Can we feed her?"

We went together to the cafeteria and got the kitten some milk and set up a nice little breakfast for her in my janitor's closet. Darren was very caring with the kitten—completely the opposite of the Darren who had been posturing as a tough guy for weeks and weeks. Now I couldn't help but think of him as this gentle, misunderstood giant with a kind heart. I mentally erased all the negative words on his report card. Together, we called the local animal shelter and made a plan for me to drop off the kitten that afternoon. This was my chance to connect with Darren.

I started out slowly. He began to talk. By the end of our time together, Darren was crying and holding his kitten closely. He told me that he used to really like school, but then "somewhere around sixth grade, I got big and tall and my teachers got scared of me." He went on to explain that they treated him differently, as if he were dangerous, so he "became who they thought I was—a thug."

I thought of all that Darren had to carry with him every day and what it would have been like to have my teachers afraid of me at the age of thirteen. It all clicked at that moment, and I knew that *this* was the real training on diversity—going to my job every day and seeing each kid as a complex individual with his or her own history; all of them shaped by race, experience, personality, environment, social interactions, and the kind of feedback they receive from the adults around them. Although Darren hadn't been given much positive reinforcement lately, he was able to give me all I needed when he said, "You see me as just 'Darren,' though, right, Ms. B?"

COLOR OUTSIDE THE LINES

Amy Cummings-Barnabi

M Y LIFE AS an educator began as a part-time teacher and assistant girls' basketball coach. Although I had a lot to learn about teaching, it was an easy transition to go from playing college basketball to working with our girls' varsity team. We were not very good, and as both a coach and a teacher, I found myself wondering constantly, "How do you teach kids how to win?"

I often wrote inspirational quotes on the board, offered Happy Meals for taking charges in a game, and read children stories like *The Little Engine That Could* or *The Velveteen Rabbit* for inspiration before a game. Still, we won only two games all season. But the kids stuck it out and seemed somewhat amused by my antics. One of my favorite quotes that I wrote on the board that year was, "You *see things* and you say, 'Why?' But I *dream things* that never were and I say, 'Why not?'" What did we have to lose? We had nowhere to go but up.

At tournament time we got the last pill, meaning the last pick. Fortunately, we were paired up against a team that didn't have a great record, and we felt our kids had as good a chance as any to win.

"I really think we can make a run in the tournament this year," Coach Mike told me one day after practice.

"We just have to get *them* to believe that," I replied.

We had played in a very tough league that year, and this was the chance for our kids to show just how much they had improved since the beginning of the season. Coach and I knew they could do it. Convincing them of that was another story.

A few nights before the game, we had a team get-together. I had the girls sign in when they walked in, and at the top of the page it read, "Color Outside the Lines. Sign in if you want to *win!*" I had no idea what I was doing, I was making this stuff up as I went along, but the kids didn't know that. I had put together a video from that season, trying to get them to focus on the fact that we *had* gotten better each and every game. The video included highlights from the movie *The Bad News Bears* as well as us missing layups and throwing away the ball. Then the video turned to the positive, going from *The Bad News Bears* to *Rocky* and *Rudy*. It showed the girls making outstanding plays, taking charges, rebounding in traffic, and hitting key shots. I was struggling to find that one thing I thought could motivate them to win a few games in tournaments. After all, in the postseason, everyone starts out with a 0–0 record. Our chances were as good as anyone's.

I had drawn particularly close to this group of kids. What few understand is that in coaching, it's not about the money you make. As with teaching, you put in a lot of time. If you divvy up the hours and divide by your actual pay, coaches make about fifteen cents an hour! What you gain coaching young kids is the same thing you gain as a teacher: the reward of knowing, for that brief moment in time, that you actually made a difference in someone's life.

Through the trials and tribulations of the season, we seemed to have grown stronger as a unit. I had grown especially fond of one player named Erica. Before the season started, I had been told that she might be a little difficult to work with. She was hard-nosed, outspoken, and stubborn, but she was one of only two seniors on the team. Erica was a leader, and our point guard, and I knew that the team would be run through her. Once I gained her confidence, she would do anything on the court that I asked. She was quick and was always asked to defend the other team's best player. Her intensity matched mine.

The week of preparation before our first tournament game passed quickly. Still unsure of exactly what to do to motivate the girls, I picked up a box of crayons at the store. As the girls filtered into the locker room for practice, I had them choose from a sixty-four-count box of Crayola crayons.

"What's this?" they asked, intrigued.

"Don't think, just pick one." I had no reason for what I was doing. I was an elementary school teacher and spent my days surrounded by the fundamental things in life like glue, scissors, and Crayola crayons.

It was fun watching the players decide which crayon to pick. Most picked their favorite color; some chose one, put it back, and then chose another. The only rules were these:

"Take this with you tomorrow and use it during school. Instead of a pencil to write your name on your paper, use your crayon. Carry it with you wherever you go, and when you see a teammate, ask her if she has her crayon."

The next day, one of my players told me that prior to boarding the bus, she'd had to call her mom to bring her crayon to school; she'd forgotten it and did not want to be without it. Another one panicked because hers had broken, so she carried both pieces around with her. They had done what I asked when they passed each other in the hall; whether it was an upperclassman or underclassman, the question was the same: "Where's your crayon?"

Like the box full of crayons, all my players were unique, bold, and strong. I wanted them to understand that each had a share in our goal, to win as many tournament games as we possibly could. I would use this activity and theory behind the crayons half a dozen times in my teaching career, both in and out of the classroom. Although each crayon project was special to me, none felt as powerful and personal as this first lesson. Little did I know that the crayon experiment would have an impact on me throughout my career. Elementary school teachers use crayons almost every day. Every time I see a child coloring with his or her crayon, my thoughts take me back to a time and place where life was new and exciting, where learning to get better at what I did was important. And it still is.

As the team loaded the bus, each of the girls showed me her crayon without asking. They all told stories of taking notes in class with the green crayon, of writing a note to their boyfriends with indigo blue or forest green, of taking a quiz with a tango orange crayon. I collected their crayons before they went out to warm up for the game, and before tip-off I talked to the girls again, not really sure what to say to them. (Of course, I wouldn't tell them this until much later!) When they assembled in the locker room and looked at me, I smiled.

"As children, life is so simple and basic," I said, and as I made eye contact with each of my players, it struck me how a team is just like a box of crayons, each player different in her own special way. I continued, "Do you remember getting that first box of crayons? Remember how they smelled? How it felt to hold them in your hands, your very own crayons?"

I was greeted with nods of agreement. I couldn't help but feel I was getting them to believe. I couldn't help but feel we had a chance to win that game.

"There were no real rules ... well, at least at first. You colored because there was paper and you had a crayon. Then life got a little more complicated, and somewhere, someone told you to start *coloring inside the lines.* Who decides that? Who said it was wrong to color *outside* the lines? When we are children, we color outside the lines, we stuff things that matter into our pockets for our moms to find. We don't hide how we feel about things from the world because we're children, and life inspires us with the simplest things, like a crayon. But as we get older, the ideals of the world change, and we start to question everything. Instead of sharing the dreams we once stuffed into our pockets, we push them further, deep down inside, until they're washed and stuck inside some dryer, like lint. Why?" I let the words echo through the locker room. "What do you have to lose? What's wrong with being unique, with being you?"

The kids looked up, more focused and with much more confidence. Teary-eyed, I suddenly saw each athlete as who she was, a young lady about to embark on a life full of challenges and excitement. It didn't hurt that Erica was nodding her head with confidence.

"Some of you panicked today when I collected your crayon. Some were broken. All were used. 'Did I use mine enough?' you thought. In life, we sometimes become tattered and broken, sometimes worn out and unsure of what direction to go. But trust in you! Deep down inside all of you are the dreams you once shared with the world. Don't be afraid. There are too many people walking around afraid, frightened, confused. Be confident! Be you! And *color outside the lines!*"

One of the girls yelled, "Think like a crayon!" as I

walked out of the locker room. It was a good icebreaker before stepping onto the floor.

The teacher in me could see that I had them. These students of mine were not only listening, they were understanding. What an empowering feeling! Now, there was noise. I heard cheers of agreement from the team and knew it was time to play ball. As the national anthem played, I looked down the line at the girls. We had a spent a long, wonderful season together. I wasn't quite ready to give it up, not yet. As we huddled together, Coach Mike gave inspiring, last minute details. As we huddled up and yelled, *"Win!"* there was a different sense in the air of what we were about to do.

We won two tournament games before losing to the team that would be the runner-up in the States. All the heartache of not winning all season was replaced by that last week's efforts. The girls had gained a confidence that no one could take away from them, and it would follow into everything else they did that year.

Later that spring, I received a graduation invitation in the mail. It was from Erica. When I stopped by her graduation party, she gave me a hug and I gave her a gift, the book *The Little Engine That Could*.

She smiled and said, "Thanks, Coach."

When I left her party later that day, I cried. They weren't the only ones who had learned a lesson about life. That year, I learned more about myself, and what kind of teacher I wanted to become, than any college course could ever teach me. I believed in myself just as each of my players had believed in herself going into that tournament. It was a confidence that would follow me the rest of my years teaching.

When I run into these girls years later, they still ask me about the crayons. Some are married now, some even have children. To this day, I remember each one of those players, whether it's while coaching in a gym, standing in a classroom teaching, or raising my own two boys. I remember how in one season, a group of young girls taught me how to win. And I'm reminded how each of us, as teachers, has the power to teach our students to color outside the lines.

THE ICK FACTOR

Damian Bariexca

Toward the end of the 1990s, when colleagues at one of my former schools approached high-level administrators regarding a request from students to start a Gay-Straight Alliance (GSA) club, the response was concise and impossible to misconstrue: "Over my dead body." The process to start an extracurricular club was pretty straightforward, and although clubs had come and gone over the past forty years due to varying degrees of interest, none of the faculty involved could remember ever hearing of a potential club being told, "You may not exist." Essentially, a group of kids was being told, "You do not have the same rights as every other student in this high school," by adults who supposedly had the kids' best educational and social-emotional interests at heart.

If you were a gay student at that time, the shortsighted

decision of an administrator might not even appear on your radar amid the daily verbal barrage of your classmates calling one another "faggot" and referring to everything they didn't like as "gay." And whether or not a club was sanctioned by the school couldn't possibly mean much to those actively targeted, and in turn bullied, because of their homosexuality, real or perceived. That being said, eventually the school's GSA did get approval and remains active a decade after its inception. Fortunately, the aforementioned administrator did not have to die for this to happen, but his choice of idiom was fairly apt: Multiple studies report that gay, lesbian, bisexual, transsexual, and questioning (GLBTQ) youth attempt suicide at rates of anywhere from double to quadruple those of their heterosexual peers. In less severe but no less significant terms, GLBTQ people have historically been marginalized, underrepresented, and misrepresented in ways that have made it very easy for others to discriminate against them.

One arena in which GLBTQ people have been most severely underrepresented has been the American school system. Whether from disapproval, ignorance, or fear of controversy, the contributions and achievements of GLBTQ individuals have rarely been celebrated or identified as being part of the GLBTQ community. Representation is important for a number of reasons, especially in schools. For one, the simple act of acknowledging the existence of GLBTQ people throughout history provides some sense of perspective to people who are too young to realize that being gay is neither new nor a fad. In addition, there are the caricatures portrayed in the media—the butch, sleeveless, flannel-wearing lesbian; and the overly effeminate, impeccably dressed gay man—that can be addressed in school, thus broadening the perceptions of our students.

GSA clubs play a role in this effort, but there is still a lack of visibility, curriculumwise, in the schools. I feel privileged that I was able to bring some of these issues to my students for discussion and analysis when I taught a class titled Multicultural Studies. It was an elective course, open to juniors and seniors, and team-taught by an English teacher (me) and a social studies teacher. Over the course of eighteen weeks we examined different ethnic, religious, and social groups within the United States and learned about many different facets of the groups, from historical issues to current events, and how they operate within and contribute to the greater fabric of American society. One unit of the course focused specifically on issues pertinent to GLBTQ people.

The material covered in this unit varied from year to year, but topics included same-sex marriage (as well as many of the related legal issues), the presence of GLBTQ people throughout American history (for which I recommend the excellent documentary *Out of the Past*), issues faced by GLBTQ youth, and the roles and functions of GSAs. We also spent time each year discussing the students' opinions on the appropriateness and necessity of covering different GLBTQ-related issues in a class like ours.

The course was reliant on discussion, but our GLBTQ studies unit always seemed even more discussion-driven than the others, due in large part to our students' desire to have an open and honest dialogue about a topic that for many of them seemed like another world. In fact, we used to begin by asking the students why they thought this unit appeared in the course curriculum at all. Responses typically focused around the usual broad themes: reducing prejudice and discriminatory acts and trying to understand "where they're coming from." When pressed, however, most of our students had difficulty articulating more specific reasons. It was usually the students who had gay relatives (or, in some cases, who identified as gay themselves) that were able to give more insightful, nuanced answers:

"My uncle has been with his partner for ten years, and they want to have a family, but they're not allowed to adopt."

"A friend of our family is gay, but he doesn't act all flamboyant like Jack on *Will & Grace*. He's just a normal guy."

"What people don't get is that we're just like everyone else in most regards, but we're seen as these crazy *things,* and that's really frustrating!"

During these discussions, my co-teachers and I welcomed any and all questions, even the ones that tended to put us on the spot a bit (for instance, "Why do we have to learn about homosexuality? Why don't we do a unit on heterosexuality?"). Thankfully, those types of questions were few and far between, and most were of a more thoughtful nature. Since this was an elective course, the students tended to be more sensitive to those issues, even if they didn't know exactly what they were. But even among this group of students who skewed toward progressive and open-minded, issues surrounding homosexuality were still a bit more taboo and uncomfortable for many of them to deal with.

In the midst of a research and discussion activity about same-sex marriage laws, one student seemed unusually anxious. Part of this activity was to designate different areas of the room as representing different opinions, and we asked our students to relocate physically based on their views on what the legal status of same-sex marriage should be. As most of the students made their way toward the position areas that supported marriage, this student sat still, then reluctantly headed over to one of the "against" areas.

My co-teacher and I began polling the class to find out what reasons the students had for their chosen positions. When I came to Anna, she immediately jumped on the defensive: "I like gay people! I don't have anything against them, really! I have friends who are gay!" As I tried to draw her back to the topic at hand, Anna seemed almost on the verge of tears when she said, "I—I think they should have all the legal rights we talked about, but you just can't call it marriage, because it's not."

My memory of Anna is that she was very progressive overall and certainly open to considering multiple perspectives on many of the topics we covered in the course. On this day, however, she drew her own line, almost apologetically, as if her "liberal cred" were at risk. Compared with the opinions of the general student body, this belief would be considered very progressive (or heretical, depending on whom you ask), but in this group, Anna was definitely in the minority; most students in her class came out in favor of full marriage benefits, including the name, for same-sex couples.

As I expected, in the ensuing discussion her classmates asked questions like "Why would you give them all the rights but not the name?" In this instance, the difference came down to Anna's personal definition of marriage: "It's between a man and a woman. If it's between two men or between two women, it's something else." When pressed for the obvious ("Well, if it's not marriage, then what is it?"), she answered, "A civil union. A domestic partnership. I … I don't know…" When Anna trailed off at the end, it almost sounded to me as if she were struggling with her own definition of marriage. It may have been an uncomfortable moment for her, but I believe that she was challenged to really think hard about what she believed and perhaps consider the validity of a viewpoint that contradicted her own. At any rate, the hugs and friendly shoulder rubs between Anna and the classmates with whom she disagreed reassured her (and me) that there were no hard feelings and that they were following our class rule of disagreeing without being disagreeable.

As a teacher, I was pleased to see Anna stand up for what she believed in, despite being among the minority in the class. In this course, rather than simply present facts for memorization and regurgitation, one of our goals was to get kids to think critically about the subject matter and to hash out their thoughts, opinions, and questions with their classmates. We strove to create a place where students could not only learn about GLBTQ issues (and to these students, almost *everything* was new information), but, more important, discuss them with peers in a non-judgmental, safe environment.

It is important to note that not all discussions came down to taking a "pro-gay" or an "anti-gay" stance. My students seemed to respond most passionately when we talked about issues facing GLBTQ teens, because these were more tangible to them. Our class learned about Harvey Milk High School and the Walt Whitman Community School, both set up specifically to serve the needs of GLBTQ students who are unable to attend their home school due to harassment or violence. After reading about the populations these schools serve, most students seemed pretty on board with the idea:

"This totally makes sense. There's no reason gay kids should have to drop out of school just because of bullies."

"I think it's great that these kids have a place to go where they're safe and they can continue their educations in peace."

The mob mentality would usually take over at that point, with everyone chiming in about how great it was that these schools existed. If we were lucky, though, we'd have at least one or two students who were a bit more savvy about the implications:

"Wait, wait, wait ... you're telling me these kids can't

go to their own schools—where they *live*—because their principals won't do anything about the bullying?"

"Why isn't the school being held accountable for dealing with the harassment instead of pretty much making these kids choose to go somewhere else?"

"This sounds an awful lot like 'separate but equal' to me..."

These were the kinds of discussions I relished. In these instances more than any other, I think even my more homophobic students stopped seeing *gay people* or *gay kids* and just started seeing *kids*. Teenagers have a pretty acute sense of social justice, and even my most conservative students would never say that bullying and harassment are acceptable. I always felt these were more constructive discussions to have, because we weren't hung up on "gay is okay" and "no, it's not." Rather, we were addressing an issue we could all agree was a problem: What is the fairest way to achieve some kind of resolution?

The design of the course asked students for their input, their opinions, and their reflections upon reading articles and viewing films that allowed them to move past the stereotypes and deal directly with the issues of intolerance, violence, and double standards applied to one particular group of American citizens. Just as our pre-unit discussions showed that most students could not give a reason why these issues could or should be studied, they also showed that most students were ignorant as to the issues themselves. For example, while they all knew that same-sex marriage was a hot-button issue, only a handful of them knew it was legal in one state (Massachusetts, at the time), even fewer knew about the existence of civil unions and domestic partnerships, and I think I could count on one hand the number of students who understood the legal, societal, and economic benefits that marriage affords people in the United States. I say this not to belittle my students, but to illustrate that their apathy was not due to a lack of caring or an active hatred of GLBTQ people; they simply had no idea the issues even existed. Once we supplied the basic historical context and facts around issues like same-sex marriage, the students drove the discussions, and while we would step in to probe or redirect, there were times when the discussion was so genuine and the passions so inflamed, I felt almost like an intruder doing so.

At times like these, I debated internally whether I should share my personal opinions on the topic. On the one hand, I certainly didn't want to influence the discussion and have students "side" with me for brownie points. On the other hand, I felt hypocritical asking my students to share their opinions so freely without doing so myself. I decided years ago that I would share my personal feelings on this topic (and others) in the course of discussion, but I frequently reminded the students that these were just my opinions and not fact, and I would frequently tell my students, "I could very well be wrong about this—I would love to hear what you think." I think that modeling openness without proselytizing went a long way toward fostering an environment of sharing. Sometimes, students would even actively seek my opinion—during one debate about the appropriateness of discussing same-sex families in the elementary school curriculum, a student asked me, "Mr. B, how would you feel about Dylan [my son] learning about this in elementary school?" I felt that to deflect the question would have been disingenuous, so I answered honestly: "Yes, I think it's important that he learn about the various types of families that exist today—not just same-sex and opposite-sex, but nuclear, extended, single-parent, and others. How many of you come from families that you feel have been underrepresented in the books you've read or stuff you've studied?" Without forcing my view on them as the "right" one, I answered honestly and was able to draw some parallels between a family structure that was unfamiliar to most of my students (same-sex parents) and some that were more familiar.

For a unit of study that focused on a group defined by sexual orientation, very little time was spent discussing sex itself, and I think quite a few of our students were surprised by this. My response to that was always the same: To do so would reduce an entire group of human beings to one personality characteristic.

I preferred crafting the discussion as not a sex issue but as one of human and civil rights (that is, state-sponsored discrimination against gays; violence and harassment against people who are, or are believed to be, gay; selective enforcement of sodomy laws; and issues surrounding the rights of marriage). You might think that talking about sodomy laws in particular would trigger the "ick" response, especially since I used to start that lesson with a request for the definition of sodomy! After the initial giggles and awkward glances, the class was usually able to cobble together an appropriate definition. My purpose here was not to shock, but rather to compartmentalize. As soon as we established a commonly agreed-upon definition, I would ask, "Can gay people perform these acts? Can straight people perform these acts?" Once we determined that, yes, both gay and straight people can perform these acts, we could put aside the sex issue and go for the meatier stuff: "In what ways, if any, should these two groups be treated differently under the law?" Students were then able to think about the legality of enforcing laws with one group of people and not others. Usually, at least a handful of students would also take the class in the direction of the legislation of sex acts between two consenting adults and how feasible they are to enforce, as well as their constitutionality. Again, more often than not, my students could see the social injustice issues a bit more clearly once we effectively removed the so-called ick factor that so many people get hung up on.

I was astounded, yet gratified, when students would tell me, "You know, I never thought about gay people as just people before taking this class." One of the activities that I felt had an enormous impact was when we invited Bonnie and Sherry from our local chapter of PFLAG (Parents, Families, and Friends of Lesbians and Gays) to come speak about their own experiences with their gay and lesbian children. I used to smile when they'd say, "Our kids are not drag queens and leather daddies, although that's usually what you see on TV when you see gay people. My son is a college student. Her daughter is a doctor. They're regular people, just like everyone in this room." Hearing these concrete examples helped our students to see beyond the stereotypes and, as my students said, see gay people as just people. Once that stigma of "otherness" was removed, or at least reduced, real discussion about human rights and civil rights could take place.

More often than not, by the end of the unit, my students reported feeling much more sensitive to, and better informed about, GLBTQ issues and how they related to their own lives, even if they themselves did not identify as GLBTQ. In addition to the "they're just people" comments, the biggest payoff for me was that my students were given access to facts and realistic portrayals of GLBTQ people that did not fall within their very narrow cultural frame of reference. Regardless of how (or even if) their opinions about GLBTQ issues changed, I was more interested in seeing my students base their opinions on factual information rather than misinformation.

At the end of the course, long after we had completed this unit and moved on through others, our students were asked to break into small groups, research a topic pertaining to any one of the groups we'd studied, and design a forty-five-to-sixty-minute lesson to be taught to children of elementary or middle school age. Invariably, at least one or two groups would ask to design a lesson on GLBTQ issues. As much as my co-teacher and I would have loved to do this, it was not possible. When we presented our cooperating teachers with the list of groups our students might cover in their classes during our pre-project planning, we were specifically and repeatedly requested to not have students teach on GLBTQ issues. We reluctantly agreed, but I always made a point of telling the class exactly why the GLBTQ unit was off-limits.

It is easy to discriminate against any group of people perceived to be significantly different from you, because as the differences become more significant, there is more room for judgment to come into play: The way *those people* do *x, y,* and *z* is gross/immoral/disgusting/wrong/not in line with what I believe to be right. From there, even passively turning a blind eye to injustices inflicted by others is easier than fighting for equality. However, when any marginalized group is humanized rather than demonized, the differences begin to seem less important than the underlying similarities we all share as human beings. People are less likely to discriminate or commit acts of violence against those they deem to be "like us." Keeping GLBTQ issues visible in the public school curriculum is important not only to the students in those classes, but also to the country as a whole, for when we decrease homophobic words and actions (along with racist, sexist, and other discriminatory acts), the greater society can only benefit.

POCKETS FULL
OF POKER CHIPS

Randy Howe

TWO TEEN MOTHERS get into a shouting match with no regard for the little children in the room. A seventh grader uses a racial epithet against her own sister. An autistic boy calls another boy the n-word in front of everyone on the basketball court. Each incident took place as I looked on—and each one helped teach me how important it is to think first before acting on behalf of a student.

When I first started teaching, I was neither experienced enough nor sensitive enough to handle such situations well. I was certified in social studies but working toward my master's in special education when I was hired to serve as the academic teacher in a program for teen mothers. There was a social worker for the girls and a nursery, right there on campus, for their babies. It was a well-run program, but we frequently hit the kinds of snags you'd expect when working with a group of girls who were sleep-deprived and had all too often been emotionally or physically abused. One such snag was arguments. Another was bullying.

"Your baby's daddy don't care 'bout bein' with you no more. He out gettin' some from everybody"—a finger pointed at the intended target—"everybody 'cept you!"

Other popular topics included, "Girl, why don't you feed that child?" And, "Why you dress your baby that way? I might be able to find you some hand-me-downs..."

They were all in the same boat, but to worry about hypocrisy was to empty your gun of precious bullets. Strike deep enough with your words and the other girl would have a hard time responding, let alone recognizing that it was the pot calling the kettle black.

One difficult situation was a love triangle of sorts. Marco was a high-school dropout who'd landed the kind of job that pays great money when you're seventeen but doesn't offer much in the way of future prospects. He did have a white Mustang, though, and from what the girls said, he looked "pretty fly behind those tinted windows."

The tension was immediate when Jamie enrolled in our program. Four months before, she'd given birth to Marco's son, and eight months before, so had Desiree. Desiree felt that she had full rights to Marco, but our social worker, Marjorie, was working to set her straight. She hoped to capitalize on Desiree's capacity for forgiveness to welcome Jamie into the program, but Des wasn't quite there yet.

"You ain't nothin' but a slut!" This came at the end of Jamie's first week, and it came ugly, right in the middle of the nursery.

"I ain't no slut," Jamie yelled back. "I been with one man. Not like you!"

We got them out of the nursery, but they were in the amphitheater now, their voices echoing loudly enough to almost drown out the cries of the infants and toddlers.

"Slut!" shouted one.

"Slut!" shouted the other. It continued, despite our pleas and negotiations.

The only way to stop it was by separating the girls, so while Marjorie backed Jamie into a corner, I picked Desiree up, pinning her arms down so she couldn't scratch me, and carried her into the girls' bathroom. We slammed through the heavy wooden door, which I let close halfway behind me.

With adrenaline pumping, I yelled, "You have got to stop yelling!"

So now it was me calling the kettle black. Nothing about this felt like teaching.

"Move yo' ass outta my way!" Desiree shouted, tears streaming down her face. Then, in a quieter, more desperate voice: "Please. I got to see my baby."

"Wait here, Des. Splash some cold water on your face." I backed out, let the door close behind me, and stared at the empty seats of the amphitheater. Desiree had suffered a traumatic brain injury and was prone to emotional outbursts. Part of her disability was forgetting about conversations and confrontations in a matter of minutes, so I was sure she would forgive me. I felt terrible about picking her up, though. To make matters worse, I could hear Marjorie and Jamie talking in calm voices across the amphitheater. Marjorie was a real pro when it came to de-escalation.

Five years later, I decided to try my hand at younger students. My new school, a K–8 magnet school in New Haven, was so small that each grade had just one class. So when two sisters, Tasia and Leelee, transferred at the beginning of seventh grade, they received the exact same schedule. Tasia had been held back in elementary school, and the mother, Ms. Yancy, came in to talk to us about the extent of their sibling rivalry.

"As you'd expect, the girls fight. And Tasia feels real bad about being in the same class as Leelee. You got to watch that girl, y'all. Leelee's the quiet type, but she knows how to make some trouble. She's really startin' to smell herself." This was a phrase the language arts teacher, Kayla, later explained to me. It meant that Leelee was beginning to assert herself, and it was not a compliment. "Tasia's got her problems in reading and she's no angel, but that Leelee sure do love to instigate. You know what I'm sayin'?"

We knew.

Kayla and I also knew that our principal was no disciplinarian. Still, her response was disappointing the first time Leelee and Tasia squared off. I was in the classroom but missed the gesture or phrase that triggered the whole thing.

"You jus' mean, Leelee. That's why Mama don't like you!"

"Yeah?" Leelee stuck out her chin and raised her eyebrows. "Why don't you go hang out with Melissa, since you such a sugar anyways."

"Oh, it's on!" Tasia wasn't playing, either. By the time I got to her, she'd already removed her coat and one of her hoop earrings. Kayla got Tasia to sit down and asked me to bring Leelee to the office. I wasn't entirely sure why until I remembered that she'd called her sister a "sugar," referring to the fact that Tasia's skin was lighter than hers. The principal called Ms. Yancy, and I was eager to hear how she would handle one of her daughters making a racist comment to the other. Half an hour later, we all gathered in the principal's office.

After Kayla finished recounting the details, the principal, seemingly oblivious to the tension in the air, said, "Seems like this is just a little disagreement between sisters."

Kayla and I exchanged pained glances. It ended up as we knew it would, with a slap on the wrist: "And I want your essays about the importance of family on my desk first thing tomorrow morning. Understood?" So out of anger, I was harsher than intended in Leelee's discipline referral. I didn't even have to write one, given that Kayla would, but I did so anyway, probably because I felt so powerless. I couldn't believe the lack of response from the principal. From Ms. Yancy, too. They acted as if a whole class hadn't been disrupted, as if another, completely innocent girl hadn't been dragged into the sister's "disagreement." There was a part of me that couldn't let it go, so I wrote about how "damaging a racial slur can be to the psyche of an individual student and to the class as a whole." I also pointed out how "disrespectful she was toward another student." I thought to write Tasia up, too, but let it go. I'd used up all I had in that one referral. I felt spent. At least until I called Leelee down to my office before dismissal. I always let students know what I'd written in their discipline referral and, more important, why. Doing so usually made for a good teachable moment, but in this case it felt more like the punishment itself. Leelee's face was frozen in an uncomfortable half smile as I read. Spitting out words like "damaging" and "disrespectful," I felt as if I were making a mistake but couldn't quite put my finger on why. Leelee said she would apologize to Melissa, then went home.

Inconsistencies continued to plague the school, and in 2006 I decided to return to high school. When my new principal, a visionary named Stan, offered me the job, I accepted immediately. During our one interview, he'd been open about viewing behavior as "an opportunity to help kids grow." Toward the end of my third week, I had the chance to see this philosophy in action.

I had been assigned all of the freshmen and sophomores on an IEP (individualized education plan), one of whom was Jamarcus, a New Haven kid who called himself a "junior" despite the fact that he was enrolled in four tenth-grade classes. Another one of my students was a freshman named Michael, who had Asperger's syndrome (a high-functioning form of autism) and came to us from a rural town north of the city.

Jamarcus started gaming me right away, doing little in his classes but assuring me, every time I tried to engage him, that all was well. So I stopped in to talk to Stan.

"He really needs a male role model," he told me. "He lives with two older foster parents he calls his grandparents. His grandfather isn't really involved, though. Maybe with your encouragement, things will go better."

A few days later, Jamarcus and Michael had a run-in during lunch. I was already impressed with the way the kids let anyone who wanted to play into their basketball games. So it was that Michael found himself trying to get away from Jamarcus's stifling defense. As Jamarcus shut off any possible path to the basket, he kept bumping Michael's hip, fouling him again and again and again and hoping to force the turnover. As I was about to step in, the ball glanced off Michael's foot and flew out of bounds. Jamarcus was cheered by his teammates and, feeling emboldened, yelled, "Why you standin' there? Go get the ball!"

Michael, his cheeks now bright red, countered with, "You get it, nigger!"

Absolute silence.

Michael was smart enough to retreat into the building while Jamarcus's friends calmed him down. Ten minutes later, I was sitting in Stan's office with one boy on either side of me.

Again, I found myself upset with a student. I had high expectations and always told them that. Sure, Jamarcus was a foster kid, and sure, he had a reading disability, but neither was a good excuse for going after a lesser opponent as hard as he did. As I had been with Ms. Yancy, I was curious to see how Stan would handle Michael's choice of words. And I didn't think that Michael was a racist, any more than I'd thought Leelee was. But Michael had used the most taboo word in the English language.

"Randy tells me there was a problem on the basketball court," Stan began, his finger tapping a slow and steady beat on the armrest of his chair. "What happened, Michael?"

"I didn't yell 'nigger'!"

Stan raised his eyebrows, and instantly Michael knew to just give up. He had defended himself by using the word his principal hadn't yet mentioned.

"Well, I didn't mean to yell it..."

"I know you didn't, Michael, but I have a school to run. I can't have kids calling each other hurtful names like that. If I let it go, everyone will think that we accept that kind of thing here, which we don't. I'm your principal, but I'm their principal, too. I'm Jamarcus's principal. Can you understand that?"

"Yes," Michael said flatly. His eyes were close to overflowing.

Jamarcus was sitting still, waiting quietly like the veteran of the principal's office that he was. Who could blame him? Within ten seconds, Michael had extracted his own confession, after all. Jamarcus was in the same old seat, but this time he was the victim. He'd won on the court, and now he was winning here.

"So, what did you see out there, before Michael yelled?" Stan asked me.

Just as every teaching book will suggest, I started with the positive, pointing out how Michael had been welcomed into a game that featured mostly upperclassmen; but then I hammered home the point about Jamarcus overplaying the man rather than the ball. I felt myself getting angry all over again. "Jamarcus, I know you know better. You bump bodies like that with anybody else and there's going to be a fight. I expect you to have more sense than that. It's lunch, not the NBA finals."

Stan turned back to Michael, talking to him about his obvious passion for the game and how it could be a healthy thing. He talked about the courage he had displayed playing with the older guys and then about how important it is to control one's anger. He actually went on so long that I thought Michael might not receive any sort of punishment, but then Stan gave him an in-school suspension for the rest of the day and the following day as well. Michael apologized, and there was a fine moment when Jamarcus accepted his handshake. After the freshman left, though, I wanted to make sure that Jamarcus understood. "You know he's lower than you on the totem pole and that he's still figuring out how to play ball. He was wrong to say what he said, but you were wrong, too. You didn't act like a man out there today, and look at what happened—"

At that moment, the bell rang. Stan thanked Jamarcus, then dismissed him to class. He nodded, though, for me to stick around.

"You need to leave him with more to go on." Before I could answer the charge, he continued. "When students walk out of this office, I want them to understand what it is they need to do, but I also want them feeling like they're capable of doing it. We have to put some poker chips back into their pockets. I let Michael know that he did something wrong, but also that I see the good in him. The potential. When Jamarcus left, his pockets were empty. He might even wonder if we're giving up on him. Without any chips, there's no reason to stay in the game."

"I have high expectations for J. I thought I let him know that much."

"You implied it, but I'm not sure he heard you. Abandoned children start life without much to go on. Throw in a disability and they're deep in debt. What he needs is for you to lend him some chips. Then, help him to pay you back."

"I understand." And I meant it. One reason I'd been willing to switch schools was that I'd learned all I could learn on my own. In my two previous schools, I was the only special education teacher and knew that I'd come to the end of my learning curve. Stan's poker-chip metaphor was exactly the kind of challenge I was looking for. "I'll follow up with him before buses."

As I got up to leave, Stan lent me a couple of poker chips, not that I even realized it at the time. "I'm glad you were out there today. I'm impressed with how quickly you've made yourself a part of our school."

I thanked him and reminded myself to try to be more objective in the future. Déjà vu all over again.

Part of being a special education teacher is replacing frustration with hope, both in the students and in yourself. The further down a kid slips, the harder you have to work to raise him or her back up. Success comes in small packages, and the growth comes in fits and starts. Most days it's one step back, with no guarantee you'll ever get to two steps forward, but that doesn't mean you stop trying. Fostering optimism is a professional responsibility and one I am still working on sixteen years into my career.

I had plenty of time to work with Jamarcus, with Michael, too, but as I walked back to my office, I thought about how the fight between Desiree and Jamie had turned physical only after I'd interceded. It seemed necessary at the time, but there had to be another way. There's always another way. For example, hindsight had shown me how badly we'd botched the Leelee-Tasia situation. From the get-go, they should have been dealt with in separate meetings. They were already lumped together enough without us adding to it. And it was okay for me to submit a discipline referral, since the general rule is the more documentation the better; but discipline referrals should never be subjective. Mine was. I should have written up Tasia, too. I should have met with her to discuss what had happened and ask about what was going on. I should have put some poker chips into each girl's pocket. As it turned out, I gave little to either girl.

Back in my office I sat down to lunch, but before eating I jotted down some things to talk to Jamarcus about, some positives to try to build on. I would do better with him than I'd done with Desiree. With Leelee and Tasia, too.

Slut. Sugar. Nigger.

In all three cases, a student went for the jugular with the harshest word he or she could think of. Kids are expected to have knee-jerk reactions. Educators are not. The things I say to my students have to be meaningful and personal, overtly supportive and subtly instructive. The poker chips have to be dished out deliberately and with purpose if I am to help them along their personal learning curves; if I am to help myself along my own learning curve as well.

■

THE LESSON'S
CLOSURE

FIVE STEPS TO DIFFERENTIATION

Mona Briggs, EdD

That students differ may be inconvenient but is inescapable. Adapting to that diversity is the inevitable price of productivity, high standards, and fairness to students.

—Theodore Sizer

I F NOTHING ELSE, the 2001 No Child Left Behind Act has required teachers, parents, and administrators to confront the ugly fact that not all children have been well served in our schools. For far too long, well-intentioned teachers have used a "shotgun" approach in classrooms—tossing out the latest program or innovation and hoping something would stick. As our classrooms have become more diverse with increasing numbers of struggling learners, we now know we must be much more strategic in our planning and instruction.

It is clear that we can no longer rely on what we have done in the past. In order to "grow" *all* learners, we must be willing to acknowledge, even celebrate, these differences. To do this, it is essential that as teachers we approach lesson planning and instruction differently. We must get over the fear that differentiation is impossible to do … that it takes too much time … that it requires too much "stuff." Hopefully, whether this is your first year in education or your forty-first (as it is for me), these recommendations will point you in a new direction that will capture your imagination, energize your work, focus your efforts, and maximize learning for your students.

- Have a broad repertoire of researched-based teaching strategies that you are comfortable implementing:
  - Inquiry-based learning
  - Cooperative learning
  - Highly effective questioning skills
  - Information-processing strategies
  - Direct instruction
  - Nonlinguistic representations
  - Learning contracts
  - Scaffolding
  - Imagery-based elaboration

- Make sure you know your students; it is one of the benefits of the fourth "r," which is "relationship-building":
  - Learning styles/preferences (kinesthetic, visual, auditory, spatial)
  - Personal interests
  - Multiple intelligences
  - Analysis of student formative and summative assessment data
  - Cultural and ethnic influences
  - Gender influences
  - Physical, emotional, social, and cognitive characteristics
  - Family characteristics/socioeconomic status
  - Readiness to learn/prior knowledge

- Change your thinking:
  - Differentiation is a philosophy—a *belief* system.
  - Come to terms with what is fair and equitable for each individual student rather than the class as a whole, understanding that equal doesn't always mean equitable.
  - Allowing students to choose ways to learn and demonstrate learning with support from the teacher is a good thing.
  - It is not okay to "teach to the middle."
  - Just as students are smart in different ways, they also learn differently.

– Students can and should think for themselves.
– Teachers should be encouraged to provide multiple assignments for students within the same classroom.
– Class activities should be structured so that each and every child is challenged to reach his or her greatest potential.
– Implementation of flexible grouping around different interests, learning styles, and levels of thinking can and should be done.
– When students are allowed to use resources, whether human, print, technological, or visual, it is not "cheating."
– Every child deserves second chances.
– Anxiety and fear do not contribute to meaningful learning; emotional safety is a prerequisite for learning.

Just Do It! Top Five Ways to Differentiate Instruction

1. Learning environment (aesthetically pleasing)
    a. Lighting options: use of lamps, back to the window, light near the desk, full-spectrum lighting
    b. Furniture that may be added to your room: small sofa, rocking chair, beanbags, reading rug, and the like
    c. Use of living plants, aquariums, and terrariums
    d. Personal space needs

e. Availability of adaptation devices
    i.   Highlighters
    ii. Pencil grippers
    iii. Erasable pens
    iv. Headphones
    v.   Laptops
    vi. Stress balls
    vii. Photocopied notes
    viii. Foot support
    ix. Tilt-top desk
    x.   Color-coded materials
f. Student's position in the classroom
    i.   Consider preferential seating, which doesn't always mean at the front of the room
    ii. Consider the students' senses (vision, hearing, smell, touch)

2. Content (the *what* of teaching: essential curriculum/ state or district standards)
    a. Level of complexity
        i.   Analyzing the information from a different perspective, extending the concept, examination from an interdisciplinary approach, introducing ethical considerations
    b. Acceleration
        i.   Individual pacing, time adjustments
    c. Novelty
        i.   Real problems, research, use of primary sources

    d. Depth
       i. Language of the discipline, understanding the rules that govern it, understanding the theory behind it
    e. Compacting
       i. Adapting the regular curriculum through elimination of work, condensing or streamlining the essential curriculum
    f. Use of abstractions
       i. Going beyond factual information to the hidden meanings, underlying ideas, or symbolism
    g. Reorganization
       i. Selecting new arrangements for the content other than chronological order

3. Process (the *how* of teaching: methods and strategies implemented)
    a. Inquiry and discovery
    b. Inductive and deductive reasoning
    c. Independent studies and self-directed projects
    d. Higher-order questioning/essential questions
    e. Action research
    f. Service learning activities
    g. Problem-based learning
    h. Tiered assignments
    i. Cooperative learning opportunities
    j. Individualized instruction/one-on-one mentoring
    k. Socratic seminars

l. Cues and advanced organizers
m. Setting objectives and providing effective feedback
n. Revising for logic, transitions, and word choice
o. Summarizing/note-taking
p. Generating and testing hypotheses
q. Comparing and contrasting

4. Participation (authentic student engagement)
    a. Adapting how the student participates
    b. Adapting how much the student participates
    c. Adapting the rules or goals for the student's participation
    d. Adapting assessments to include grading on individual growth

5. Product (end result of the learning sequence)
    a. Role-play
    b. Lab report/experiment
    c. Debate/panel discussion
    d. Mural
    e. Interview(s)
    f. Simulation
    g. Oral report
    h. Diary
    i. Video
    j. PowerPoint presentation
    k. Photo essay
    l. Illustrated story/political or editorial cartoon
    m. Models

n.   Brochure

o.   Portfolio

p.   Choral reading

q.   Research/case study

r.   Position paper

s.   Glossary

t.   Scrapbook

u.   Mini-teach

v.   Skit (example: public service announcement)

w.   Script for a play

x.   Illustration/poster/flip books

REFERENCES

Blaz, D. (2008). *Differentiated Assessment for Middle and High School Students*. Larchmont, NY: Eye on Education.

Heacox, D. (2001). *Differentiating Instruction in the Regular Classroom: How to Reach and Teach All Learners, Grades 3–12*. Minneapolis, MN: Free Spirit Publishing.

Marzano, R. (2003). *What Works in Schools: Translating Research into Action?* Alexandria, VA: Association for Supervision and Curriculum Development.

Tomlinson, C. (1995). *How to Differentiate Instruction in the Mixed Ability Classroom*. Alexandria, VA: Association for Supervision and Curriculum Development.

Turville, J. (2008). *Differentiating by Student Preferences*. Larchmont, NY: Eye on Education.

Wormeli, R. (2006). *Fair Isn't Always Equal: Assessing and Grading in the Differentiated Classroom*. Portland, ME: Stenhouse Publishers.

READING QUESTIONS

1. What does the title of this book mean to you in your work with children? In turn, how do you define "differentiated instruction"?

2. After reading Amy Beth Blumstein's "The Power of Words," how would you have responded to Ikram's mother if she tried to pull her son out of your class? How would you have responded to the headmaster when he told you to put professional responsibility ahead of personal concern, even in the wake of 9/11? How do you define professionalism, especially when challenged or questioned by others?

3. In thinking about the patience required to teach Take-hiro how to speak ("The Memorable One"), Glen how to write his name ("Oh Yes, He Can!"), and Becky ("Something's Gotta Give"), Mark ("The Bodyguard"), Jamarcus ("Pockets Full of Poker Chips"), and Blake ("The Star, A Heart Within") how to behave in school, are you reminded of a certain student who tested your patience? What was it you saw in that child

that helped you to be so patient? Should it even be considered patience, or is it just part of the job?

4. In Lisa Santilly's work with deaf and hard-of-hearing students ("When Dogs Can Talk"), she often has to scrap her lesson and embrace the teachable moment. How do you strike the balance between curricular needs and the immediacy of student curiosity? When the lesson has to take priority over a student's question, how do you make sure to return to that topic so as not to discourage HOTS (higher-order thinking skills)?

5. What are some of the concerns that the authors have about English language learners (ELL) when describing their work with Miguel ("First Row, Second Seat Back") and Tony ("*La Oportunidad*")? What do you see as the future for ELL education?

6. In "Pockets Full of Poker Chips" (Randy Howe) and "Unconditional Dedication" (Erica C. Aguirre), the authors honestly depict the difficulty they had compromising between their ideas about teaching and the abilities of their students. How have you had to compromise? And what was most difficult about making those adjustments to your approach and expectations?

7. In "What My Students Taught Me" (Allison Anderson) and "Beyond Boxes: How Today's Students

Disable Labels" (Kerstin Rowe), the authors describe how humor and dialogue helped bridge the racial gaps that existed, or were thought to exist, in their classrooms. How do you decide what is appropriate, humor- and conversationwise, with your kids, especially with respect to sensitive issues? Have you ever been burned by a student, caregiver, or administrator who didn't appreciate a joke or comment that was made in your classroom?

8. In Dr. Samuel R. Bennett's "Steven and Me," a teacher goes above and beyond with one particular student. What are the risks when helping a student outside of the classroom, whether it is giving the child something or bringing him or her somewhere? What stands to be gained, and how much did this weigh into Dr. Bennett's decision, in your opinion?

9. Drs. Rebecca Branstetter, Susan DeMersseman, and Kathy Briccetti are all school psychologists who have very limited time to positively impact a student's life. In your district, have school psychologists and social workers been cut due to budgets that failed to pass? What kind of impact did this have? What are your recommendations for the kinds of counseling that should be available to meet the needs of today's students?

10. Although there are many teacher stories in this collection, there are also quite a few from other

professionals, including school psychologists and even a student teacher. In "Color Outside the Lines," Amy Cummings-Barnabi writes about a basketball coach's desperation shot of an attempt to get her players to believe in themselves. What can classroom teachers learn from lessons like these? How do they apply to the different kinds of learners and personality types in your classroom? Did you ever attempt something out of blind hope and have it work out?

11. In "The Power of One," Dr. Kathy Briccetti tries to undo a cultural standard in certain families: hitting back if someone hits you. Have you had to contend with this kind of conflict? And if so, how did you try to point the student in the right direction while being respectful of the caregiver at home?

12. Dr. Mona Briggs writes about the best ways to differentiate instruction in the closing piece of *One Size Does Not Fit All*. Which of these suggestions have you used successfully, and which have not been of benefit to the students despite your best efforts? Are there any that you are planning to try in your classroom?

13. Susan Laughlin's story reveals how Japanese culture frowns on individuality; thus the title "The Nail That Sticks Up Gets Hammered Down." Is it possible to respect individuality while enforcing conformity in order to get through a lesson or activity? What is a

favorite memory you have of an individual student, or teacher, who simply refused to be "hammered down"?

14. Cathryn Soenksen thought of Miguel as an "irritation"; Randy Howe worried that Jamarcus was a cruel opportunist; Megan Highfill felt challenged by Jasmine's proselytizing; Erica C. Aguirre was so annoyed at Joey that she took to referring to him by his last name. Remembering a time when you were at wits' end with a student, how did you turn a negative into a positive? If you were unable to, what got in the way?

15. Jeff Ballam and Damian Bariexca write about gay, lesbian, bisexual, transsexual, and questioning (GLBTQ) students and their growing visibility in schools today. Have you had to address gender issues and sexual preference in your teaching? Was it part of the curriculum, something you decided to make part of a unit, or a response to a student question?

16. Given the current concern about teacher preparation programs, not to mention programs that provide an alternative (some might say "shortcut") route to certification, which stories in this book could be used as case studies in the teaching of classroom management? Also, in your experience, or from your professional reading, are peer programs like the one featured in Dr. Kathy Briccetti's "The Power of One" effective? Why or why not?

17. In Megan J. Koonze's "Teens on the High Seas," a girl with ADHD breaks out of her shell after a two-night field trip. What alternative-type activities have you been a part of that helped students build confidence and come into their own, so to speak? In addition, what is your all-time favorite "turnaround" story, in terms of a student who really turned it all around for him- or herself?

18. Dr. Susan DeMersseman has a bizarre, heart-wrenching conversation with Tina in "Diamonds in the Rough." What was the hardest conversation you ever had with a student? How did you approach the student's situation, and how were you able to help? On the other hand, in that same story Darren gives Dr. DeMersseman a compliment. What was the nicest thing a student ever said to you? And why do you treasure those words?

19. Making assumptions is always risky, and Kerstin Rowe, Damian Bariexca, Megan Highfill, and Lisa Santilly all touch on this in their stories. Did you ever make an assumption about a student, or group of students, that you later regretted? What did you learn from this situation?

20. In *One Size Does Not Fit All*, we see how teachers and students are held accountable. Do we also learn anything about parent accountability? What are the

keys to holding parents accountable? And is it even worth pursuing?

21. What does the future hold for students with diverse intellectual, physical, and emotional strengths and weaknesses in our schools? Will concepts such as differentiated instruction ever fully catch on, or is there something better out there that has yet to be discovered? What might that approach be? Or do you predict a return to some former initiative in order to meet the needs of kids with alternative learning styles?

22. After you read *One Size Does Not Fit All,* was there a certain student from one of the stories who remained in your thoughts? Why was that? Was it because you were reminded of a student of your own? Why is it that the most troubled—and troubling—students are often the ones we remember most?

About the Editor

RANDY HOWE lives in Madison, Connecticut, with his wife, two children, cat, and dog. And yes, there is a white picket fence.

Randy has worked in schools since 1994, when he was hired as an assistant teacher in a program for emotionally disturbed children. Since that time, he has taught GED to adults and to teens enrolled, usually via court order, in the National Guard's ChalleNGe program. He was the academics teacher in a teen parenting program at Putnam/Northern Westchester BOCES and then the special education teacher and Pupil Personnel Team chairperson at the MicroSociety Magnet School in New Haven, Connecticut. At the time of publication, Randy was in his fourth year at the Sound School, a vocational-aquacultural school on New Haven Harbor. He used his story, "Pockets Full of Poker Chips," as an opportunity to reflect on the last three schools—specifically, what he has learned about student behavior and how he can best remediate it while helping to build the student's self-esteem.

Randy graduated from Hobart College in 1993 with certification in social studies. Next came a Master of

Professional Studies in special education from Manhattanville College. In 2001 he earned an advanced certification in Educational Leadership from Teachers College, Columbia University. The following year, he began writing a weekly philosophy article for McGraw-Hill's college division; his first book was *Flags of the Fifty States and Their Incredible Histories,* followed by *The Quotable Teacher.* Other education-related books include *Teacher Haiku, A+ Educators, 101 Ways to Adjust to High School, Word Source, Speak to Me!, Here We Stand,* and *First Year Teacher: What I Wish I'd Known My First 100 Days on the Job.* He has also written about history, politics, and sports, publishing both books and trivia card sets on these topics. He had his dream come true not once but twice when he was interviewed on National Public Radio (NPR) stations in Boston and Wisconsin.

To learn more, visit *www.randyhowe.net.* There is a "One Size Does Not Fit All" group on Facebook, dedicated not just to this book, but also to the issues of diversity that exist in schools. Randy invites all to join and is also available for questions and feedback at diversitybook@ hotmail.com.

About the Contributors

ERICA C. AGUIRRE contributed "Unconditional Dedication" to *One Size Does Not Fit All.* The story takes place in her second year of teaching seventh-grade social studies, a year in which she was the veteran teaching in her small learning community. She is now in her third year of teaching.

ALLISON ANDERSON wrote "What My Students Taught Me" after fifteen years of teaching middle and high school students in New Jersey. She is also an adjunct professor of history at County College of Morris.

JEFF BALLAM, who has his Master of Arts degree, is the voice behind "The Election of 2008." It is his first published piece of writing. Mr. Ballam has been a teacher at Monte Vista Elementary, in Los Angeles, California, for twenty-six years. Currently, he teaches fifth grade and is the gifted and talented program coordinator.

DAMIAN BARIEXCA taught high school English for eight years before becoming a school psychologist. At the time of publication, he was in his second year working in that capacity, at North Hunterdon High School in Annandale, New Jersey. One of his responsibilities there is as coadvisor of the Gay-Straight Alliance. Mr. Bariexca also contributed a piece titled "Alleviating ShakesFear" to Kaplan's *The Teachable Moment*. He blogs at "Apace of Change" (*http://www.apaceofchange.com*) and can be followed on Twitter (*http://www.twitter.com/damian613*).

STEPHANIE BELL, author of "The Memorable One," is a doctoral student at Western Connecticut State University. For the past sixteen years, she has been an elementary school teacher at Increase Miller, which is in the Katonah-Lewisboro School District in New York. Other writing credits include an article for *The Clearing House* journal on project-based learning.

SAMUEL R. BENNETT, EdD, began his professional career as a police officer and is now dean of the College of Education at Southeastern University. In between, he spent twenty years in the classroom, and it was as a teacher that he met the star of his story "Steven and Me." While working with students like Steven, Dr. Bennett was selected as the Polk County Teacher of the Year, and in 2006 he was named Florida Teacher of the Year. That same year, he was one of four finalists for National Teacher of the Year.

AMY BETH BLUMSTEIN is a fifth-grade English language arts teacher at Bruno M. Ponterio Ridge Street School. She has been a teacher for fourteen years and has taught in both the United States and the United Kingdom. Ms. Blumstein is also the author of a children's book, *Jamie and Tallulah*.

REBECCA BRANSTETTER, PhD, is a school psychologist and a licensed clinical psychologist. She is currently employed by the Oakland Unified School District and has worked in Bay Area schools for eight years. She is also the CEO of Grow Assessment and Counseling Services. Dr. Branstetter contributed "The Invisible Knapsack" to *One Size* after editing a companion book, also available from Kaplan, titled *The Teachable Moment: Seizing the Instants When Children Learn*. In addition, she writes about her experiences with kids in her blog, Notes from the School Psychologist, which can be found at *www.studentsgrow.blogspot.com*.

KATHY BRICCETTI, PhD, has been a school psychologist for twenty-five years and wrote "The Power of One." She is also the author of a memoir, *Blood Strangers*, which is due to be published by Heyday Books in 2010. Dr. Briccetti's website is *www.kathybriccetti.com*.

MONA BRIGGS, EdD, contributed a different kind of chapter to *One Size* with her well-researched piece on differentiated instruction, "Five Steps to Differentiation."

PATRICIA M. CASTELLONE, author of "The Star, A Heart Within," is a third-grade teacher with degrees in elementary education, special education, and literacy. She is also an NBPTS (National Board for Professional Teaching Standards) nationally board-certified teacher. Ms. Castellone has been teaching for eight years.

JOHANNA CHESSER, the author of "Oh Yes, He Can!", is a first-grade teacher at East St. John Elementary School. She is in her fourth year of teaching.

ANNE DANDRIDGE CONRAD is the author of "Something's Gotta Give." Currently, she teaches third grade, but over the past thirty-seven years, Anne has taught fourth grade, fifth grade, and a fourth-grade/fifth-grade combination class.

AMY CUMMINGS-BARNABI is the coach behind "Color Outside the Lines." Although she no longer coaches, Ms. Cummins-Barnabi does teach social studies, reading, and language arts to sixth graders at Claymont Intermediate School. This is her thirteenth year in the classroom. She blogs at *http://thewiifitprojecttm.blogspot.com.*

SUSAN DeMERSSEMAN, PhD, contributed "Diamonds in the Rough" to *One Size Does Not Fit All.* She is a frequent contributor to the "Home and Garden" section of the *San Francisco Chronicle* and to the *Christian Science Monitor* as well as other magazines, newspapers, and books, including *Wisdom of Our Fathers,* edited by Tim Russert. Dr. DeMersseman has been a school psychologist for over thirty years.

MEGAN HIGHFILL, the author of "Anthem," has her Bachelor of Music and Master of Science in curriculum and teaching. For three years, she has taught general music in grades K–6 at Nieman Elementary School in Shawnee Mission, Kansas.

MEGAN J. KOONZE contributed "Teens on the High Seas," a story about just one of the unique experiences she's had as a high school English teacher at the Sound School in New Haven, Connecticut. Ms. Koonze has been teaching for six years and is also an adjunct composition instructor at Southern Connecticut State University.

SUSAN LAUGHLIN is a fifth-grade teacher and the author of "The Nail That Sticks Up Gets Hammered Down," a story that recounts the teaching experiences she has had across the country and around the world. She has been teaching for seventeen years.

SHAWNA MESSINA, who contributed the story "The Bodyguard," is a fifth-grade literacy teacher at Lowery Road Elementary. She has been teaching for ten years. Ms. Messina was the Outreach Communications Reading Chair for the Fort Worth Independent School District in 2008–2009 and won the district's Primary Teacher of the Year award.

KERSTIN ROWE, MEd, wrote "Beyond Boxes: How Today's Students Disable Labels" for *One Size*. Currently, her days are spent either at home with her three-year-old daughter or outside the home teaching fitness classes to adults. Ms. Rowe taught English for twelve years in schools from Benin, West Africa, to Denver, Colorado.

MADELINE SANCHEZ penned *"La Oportunidad"* while she was student teaching. Her perspective as a former English as a second language (ESL) student preparing to become an ESL teacher stands out as different in a book that is all about difference.

LISA SANTILLY earned her Honours Bachelor of Arts and Bachelor of Education (Primary/Junior), as well as her Diploma of Deaf and Hard of Hearing Education, from York University in Toronto, Ontario. She taught in Toronto, the setting of her story, "When Dogs Can Talk," for three years.

CATHRYN SOENKSEN, a teacher for twenty-five years, wrote "First Row, Second Seat Back." She teaches ninth-grade English and AVID (Advanced Via Individual Determination), a college readiness program.

ACKNOWLEDGMENTS

I WOULD LIKE TO THANK Michael Sprague, Matthew Laird, and Kate Lopaze, as each played an important part in the conceptualization, development, and production of this book. I would also like to thank Maureen McMahon for her support, mainly those insightful e-mails that always seem to arrive when I need them most.

Next, a tip of the cap of collegiality to Rebecca Bell Branstetter, whose book *The Teachable Moment: Seizing the Instants When Children Learn* can be considered a companion piece to this one and is well worth the read. Although we are on opposite coasts, traveling down the editorial road was a much smoother ride with her by my side!

Finally, just as libraries are full of books, my heart is full of appreciation for Alicia Solis, who makes it possible for me to moonlight as a writer while also balancing motherhood and a career of her own. Our children, Noelle and David, are lucky to have such a role model.

Made in the USA
Columbia, SC
14 May 2018